5.20.79

Constituent and Pattern in Poetry

Constituent and Pattern in Poetry

by Archibald A. Hill

University of Texas Press, Austin & London

Library of Congress Cataloging in Publication Data

Hill, Archibald A
  Constituent and pattern in poetry.

  Includes index.
  1. Poetics. 2. Poetry—History and criticism.
I. Title.
PN1042.H46   809.1   75–32582
ISBN 0–292–72010–6

Contents

Introduction

The reader is entitled to an explanation of the title chosen for this volume, since he may wonder why I did not use a title containing the word *structural*, since that is a term now fairly widely used in criticism. It is true that I am concerned·with patterns and structures, but I wish to use an approach to literature which differs from what is currently meant by structuralism. Here is a typical definition of structuralism as usually practiced:

> Structuralism is thus based, in the first instance, on the realization that if human actions or productions have a meaning there must be an underlying system of distinctions and conventions which makes this meaning possible. Confronted with a marriage ceremony or a game of football, for example, an observer from a culture where these did not exist could present an objective description of the actions which took place, but he would be unable to grasp their meaning and so would not be treating them as social or cultural phenomena. The actions are meaningful only with respect to a set of institutional conventions. Wherever there are two posts one can kick a ball between them but one can score a goal only within a certain institutionalized framework.[1]

The statement I have quoted from Jonathan Culler is just and penetrating, and I do not wish to quarrel with it. Culler wishes to treat the work of literature as part of a larger, meaningful system, and it is this larger system which is for him the most important type of structure. For me, on the other hand, it seems axiomatic that the work of literature is itself a structure, and for this intraliterary structure I use the term *pattern*. Like any patterns, those found in literature are composed of parts in a more or less symmetrical relationship to each other. For the parts, essentially discrete and usually sequentially arranged, I borrow the linguistic term *constituent*. In linguistic analysis, the constituents of a sentence are hierarchically arranged parts, the larger being called "immediate constituents," and the smaller, "ultimate constituents." Thus one immediate constituent in the sentence "The Greeks created democracy" is the subject, "The Greeks." The ultimate constituents of the subject, in turn, are the words and word-elements, that is, "The," "Greek," and "-s." I could, perhaps, have used the more familiar term *component*, but that term has the disadvantage of not designating a clearly discrete entity. Thus we can say that one of the components of *Gulliver's Travels* is misanthropy, but we could hardly say that misanthropy is one of its constituents.

My title, *Constituent and Pattern in Poetry*, is not meant to disagree with the position of those literary critics who call themselves structuralists. I mean only to define an approach to patterns within literature, in the belief that these patterns must be fully understood before it is profitable to try to fit the literary work into the larger structures of cultural systems and values. That is, Culler's observer should first understand such constituents as players, kicks, balls, and goal posts before he tries to fit the football game into the whole philosophical and cultural pattern of sports.

The statements and discussions which make up this volume stem from a long-standing interest, begun when I was a graduate student and matured through many lively exchanges with students and colleagues. In my years as a beginner, training in the English language was directed solely to the explication of older literature and almost nothing else. The training was relevant to *Beowulf*, certainly, but was often resented by those who wished to spend their scholarly efforts on Mark Twain. It seemed to me then, and has ever since, that linguistics should be not only a handmaiden to literature but also a study of how mankind uses language and what its nature and structure are. There has been great recent progress in achieving just this kind of linguistics, and it has been my great happiness to share some small part in that progress. No one would deny, however, that plenty of work and investigations still remain. Yet now, most universities have independent departments of linguistics at the same time that most departments of English have members well trained in the English language, contemporary as well as medieval. That particular battle has been won.

The battle which has not been won is demonstration that an adult linguistics not only can be of use to the critic of literature but also is a necessary basis without which much that he may say is open to objection and that linguistic knowledge is a tool which should always be in his kit, not to be used without caution of course and, equally of course, not his only tool and not a tool for the critic alone. Linguistics, in short, is a tool for all who wish to understand man, and the understanding that it promises is a goal for all of us who study humane letters. There has been progress toward this kind of tolerance and understanding, but the notion of linguistics as a narrow specialty having little to do with literary study remains.

As an illustration of this belief, I can quote a recent exchange in *College English*, one of the widely read periodicals dealing with English studies. The exchange is "On the Role of Linguistics in the Practice of Criticism," by Elias Schwartz and Keith Schap. Schap begins with an attack on an earlier piece by Schwartz in which Schwartz maintained that linguistics is of no use to the critic and student of literature. Schap quotes from the earlier essay: "This function [of language in literature] is not marked in the language so used; it inheres rather in the relation of that language to the total structure of the poem, a structure which is aesthetic not linguistic. There is no such thing as a distinctive literary language. And if this is true, it means that, though linguists may tell us a great deal about language, they can tell us nothing about literature."[2]

Schap defends the usefulness of linguistics to the critic, but I shall not quote him since it seems to me that in certain ways, particularly in his insistence that only Chomskyan linguistics is literarily valuable and that all non-Chomskyan linguistics is mere taxonomy, Schap is also open to criticism. At any rate, Schwartz has the last word in rebuttal, where he says, "Schap fails to confront the main point of my essay: that because the linguist regards the literary work as a piece of language, he cannot do anything but linguistic analysis of it."[3]

It is, unfortunately, not to be wondered at that much linguistic analysis of literature seems irrelevant to the critic, and it is not hard to sympathize with Professor Schwartz. That is, a linguistic study of literature which elaborately classifies the sounds of poetry, the vocabulary of poetry, or even the grammar and syntax of poetry has no relevance at all unless the items so classified are brought to bear on meaning. It is that use of linguistic classification which I have tried to demonstrate in all that follows.

First, the negative aspect of linguistic knowledge is important. That is, since all the English-speaking world knows our language, it is easy to suppose that every English speaker is as expert on his language as he is expert in it. Each such expert speaker has a tendency to believe that he is qualified to speak about the language without any special training or any knowledge of method. Unfortunately, a widespread set of beliefs and attitudes which constitutes a pseudolinguistics exists, leading only to false conclusions. A good example of this pseudolinguistics is cited in the last chapter, "Figurative Structure and Meaning." There, a critic, in discussing the last four lines of Emily Dickinson's poem "The Soul selects her own Society," says only one open vowel is found in the lines and bases his aesthetic conclusion on that supposition. By my count, however, the vowels whose occurrence is restricted are close rather than open; so the critic's conclusion is groundless.

Of course, other fallacies can be discovered when fallible human beings write about literature. Among them are failing to choose consistently in the use of Occam's razor and falling into the trap of circularity. Avoidance of such pitfalls is not the particular virtue of linguistics but rather of sophisticated analytical method wherever practiced. I shall therefore say little about it here, though I have tried in all the essays given to make steady use of the argument of simplicity, or parsimony of hypotheses, sometimes, perhaps, to the exasperation of my readers. In general, however, negative usefulness of linguistic knowledge or of sophistication of method is not sufficient to convince; positive demonstrations of usefulness alone can do so. In consequence, these essays regularly include a reasonably full analysis of a poem or poems, according to the method which I believe to be most suitable, always directed toward understanding the totality of meaning and aesthetic effect.

It is worthwhile, I believe, to outline the principal ideas that are developed in the essays and to outline their growth as I continued working in this chosen field. One idea is general and is perhaps that which I hold most firmly. It is that literature is a human activity and, like all human activity, capable of being analytically investigated with human intelligence. Further, I believe equally strongly that if such investigation increases our understanding of literature, it is worth practicing. Another general idea that I strongly hold is that the method of literary investigation, when properly carried out, must not only rest on a linguistic base but also go beyond it. The method thus becomes one specifically designed for literary investigation, not merely for the investigation of casual speech. Thus the method I have striven to develop is analytic and linguistically based but also directed, above all, to works of literature considered as individual and organized wholes.

When these general ideas are stated, there remain a number of more detailed ideas, some of which developed somewhat gradually as I worked. The first such idea falls to some extent outside the scope of the present volume since it concerns the relation of phonology and verse, a subject treated only incidentally in these essays. The idea, or belief, was that a knowledge of the phonological patterns of English speech and their meanings could often be brought to bear on poetry so as to aid in understanding either the meaning or the aesthetic effect of poems. The only example of the coincidence of verse structure and phonology, and of both to meaning, which is included is in a short passage from Gerard Manley Hopkins, namely, the "dapple-dawn-drawn Falcon" of *The Windhover*.

Probably the next idea, in terms of time of development, is an appreciation of pattern and design in poetry and the way in which an examination of the design can lead to recovery of meaning. The discussion of such poems as *Tell me where is fancie bred*, and that of two of Emily Dickinson's poems in the last essay in this volume, develops the idea that a partial discovery of design in meaning can be used to recover remaining portions. This idea is used throughout the essays.

Another one of the ideas developed fairly early was the realization that the structures of language limit the types of external poetic structures practiced in any given community. Thus one essay discusses the impossibility of rhyme in Japanese poetry since the number of permitted final sounds is so limited that rhyme is all-pervasive and cannot therefore be used as an added ornament.

A strong formative influence on these essays came from a paper by George L. Trager, "The Field of Linguistics," in 1949. His paper was a mapping of the total field of linguistics into three levels: a prelinguistic, a microlinguistic, and a field beyond the upper border of language—that of meaning in the sense of correspondence between linguistic items and items in the nonlinguistic world. This area he somewhat unfortunately called the area of metalinguistics, a term that led to confusion with quite different earlier uses of the term. I have made full use of his map of the several areas but have avoided his terminology. I was struck with the idea that the field of literary study could be similarly mapped into three levels, though not in exact correspondence to the levels of language. That is, Trager's prelinguistic level of acoustics and articulations is irrelevant to literature, and the microlinguistic level of vocabulary, grammar, and syntax forms part of the preliterary level in studying literature. The idea is most fully developed in "Poetry and Stylistics" but is background for many of the essays. It has been of use in formulating literary theory in that it defines the place of linguistics in literary study.

Probably the most important formative influence comes from Martin Joos, who gave a paper before the Linguistic Society of America in 1953—"A First Theorem in Semantics." In this paper he formulated the law of least lexical contribution to meaning and its converse, the law of maximal contextual contribution. I have used the concept steadily in all the essays written since 1953. I can scarcely cite all the instances of use in this book, but at least four essays are conspicuous examples. They are "Analogies, Icons, and Images," "Principles Governing Semantic Parallels," "Some Points in the Analysis of Keats's *Ode on a Grecian Urn*," and "Imagery and Meaning: A Passage from *Lycidas* and a Poem by Blake." Of these, the first gives a full statement of the law with proper reference to Joos's various formulations of it. The others offer various corollaries to the law, such as when a meaning suggested by a wider context differs from one suggested by a narrower context, it is the wider context that takes precedence. The essay on John Keats makes use of the law not only in an attempt to solve the famous crux in the conclusion "Beauty is truth" but also in solution of a difficulty in the meaning of the first line. In discussing William Blake's *London*, I proposed a second corollary;

namely, that when we have a choice between a less and a more precise meaning, the more precise meaning is to be preferred. The essay on Blake, moreover, makes use of a slight twist in the method of using the Joos law; that is, it is possible to blot out the word being investigated and then ask oneself, or a jury, what would be the most probable way of filling the resultant blank. If the relationship of the blank filler and the actually presented word or words can be established, we have an obviously useful semantic tool.

Two other theoretical statements complete the final structure of methodological ideas for interpretation. The first of these is use of a simple probability theory. The idea arose in a way that is only partly given in the essay "Principles Governing Semantic Parallels." I had been involved in a semipublic argument with a friend and colleague over the interpretation of a poem by Robert Frost. As many critics do, my friend wished to interpret the poem with the maximum of concrete imagery. For instance, he proposed that "roar" applied by Frost to the noise of wind was to be taken as a definite reference to a lion. I won the argument by a *reductio ad absurdum*, making the whole poem a series of zoological references and leading to the conclusion that Frost was suffering from delirium tremens. At the end, however, I found that my burlesque was frightening. I could establish that the interpretation was absurd only because I had deliberately made it up to be so—I could not point to the fallacy which I had deliberately committed. The result, finally, was formulation of the importance of clustering and, above all, of ordered clustering in any interpretation based on analogical parallelism. Randomly ordered, isolated parallels are worth nothing in such interpretations and actually can be interpreted as situations in which the probability of meaningful interpretation goes down with each added item. Such a fallacious interpretation of parallels is one that I have recently seen, in which the sources of the imagery of Hopkins's *Windhover* are attributed to Shakespeare's *Henry V* by such parallels as that the king disguised himself to find out the state of his army's morale, while Hopkins speaks of "My heart in hiding"; Bardolph's nose is fiery, and Hopkins speaks of "the fire that breaks from thee then"; Bardolph steals what is probably a pyx, which is adorned with gold, and Hopkins speaks of coals gashing themselves "gold-vermilion."[4] The fallacy here is perhaps extreme, but simpler examples of it are all too common.

The last idea in the battery is that formation of a line of verse is in all probability preceded by an utterance, fragmentary perhaps, but in normal language. This underlying utterance is then transformed into the deviant form characteristic of poetic style. The statement just made is not always understood and does not mean that the poet lisps in syllogisms before the numbers come. The theory is dependent on a belief, which I firmly hold, that any organized thought is essentially a linguistic process. If the theory is correct, recovery of any underlying normal utterances is an important tool in the recovery of meaning. The theory is developed in the analysis of a syntactic crux in the *Ode on a Grecian Urn*, where it proved useful in disposing of considerable amounts of critical ink spilled to little purpose. The theory was also applied to a poem of E. E. Cummings in the essay "Two Views of Poetic Language and Meaning: The Poem as Cryptogram and as Example of Deviant Grammar." It must be said, however, that Cummings is the sort of exception that can be said to prove the rule—his deviance seems to be a deliberate and even mechanical distortion, whereas most poets modify normal language for poetic purposes rapidly, subconsciously, and with their goal set as exactness of meaning or enhancement of aesthetic effect, not as the construction of cryptograms.

These, then, are the full set of tools and ideas which I have tried to develop for analytical purposes in the study of literature. It will be noted that almost all of the essays follow the same pattern. I have tried to state the proposed theoretical principle first and then test it against the analysis of a particular poem. In all instances I have endeavored to focus the principles and their uses on the recovery of meaning or explication of an aesthetic effect, since only in this way can the relevance of analytical method be demonstrated. Incidentally, I do not much care whether the methodology I have tried to develop is called linguistic, critical, or something else. My own preference is to call it simply analytical, and my hope is that it is a method specifically suited to the subject matter investigated, namely, literature.

As well as pointing out the general principles that have been made use of in this collection of essays, I think it is useful to describe, at least briefly, the principles of selection and organization which governed the choice of essays for reprinting. When all the essays on literary subjects which I had written were laid out on my desk, it was clear that they would have produced a swollen and formless body, probably calculated to discourage most readers. As a result, with some urging from the University of Texas Press, fourteen essays were omitted and only twelve selected. The twelve here given are unified, at least somewhat, in a number of ways. First, they all concern short poems, since these form the most readily accessible testing grounds for analytical procedures. Second, all are concerned with poems as designs, and all fit into a thought-out scheme of the relations of literature and language.

I have pointed out that I owe a great deal to two friends and fellow workers in linguistics, George L. Trager and Martin Joos. I should add that I owe a more general, but none the less important, debt to the work of a great linguist of a former generation, Leonard Bloomfield, whose writings led me to a realization of the dangers in an explanation of literature that relies on such mentalistic concepts as "author's intention" and gave me a firm realization that it is always necessary to work from the more knowable to the less knowable, rather than to attempt the reverse. I cannot close this list without mentioning one other colleague of many years' standing, the late Bernard Bloch, from whom I got much in the way of close observation in phonology, and with whom I carried on many discussions and arguments, enlightening because the light was never covered by too much sweetness. And, last, I think that I owe, not to any single individual, but to all my mentors, friends, and students the realization that no necessary conflict exists between art and science—both are models of human experience, and both lead to an increase of understanding.

Part One
The Definition of Literature and the
Study of Its Patterns

Chapter One
A Program for the Definition of Literature

The essay which follows is frankly programmatic, not a report of experimentation or research which has been already performed. In a number of ways it will seem to offer no more than a somewhat ponderous and formalistic technique for arriving at results parallel to those that most people arrive at more easily by common sense. For this I offer no apology, since my basic assumption is that rigorous analysis often consists in restatements of processes usually carried out nonrigorously and intuitively, and objection to restatement is therefore no more than objection to rigorous analysis itself.

I should offer as a suggestion that most definitions of literature start from a characteristic corpus of utterances, the "institutionalized great books," which are characteristic of Western culture and a good many others. For us these institutionalized great books contain the works of men like Homer, Vergil, Dante, Cervantes, Shakespeare, and Goethe. It is almost mandatory to accept these works both as examples of literature par excellence and as examples of literary virtue. For instance, it seems to me doubtful that anyone could hold a position in an English department and let it be known that he considered *Hamlet* as either nonliterary or bad literature. Under such circumstances the typical essay written on one of these works is an explanation of why it is great literature, not a consideration *ab initio* of whether it is in fact an example of literature. Again, tacitly, a given work before us is judged to be an example of literature by whether or not it shares observable characteristics with one of the institutionalized great books. The procedure is wise and enables us to say that, whether we like it or not, *Abie's Irish Rose* is literature because it resembles *Hamlet* and that the *Ormulum* is literature because it resembles Homer and Vergil.

Such processes of definition are separate, of course, from rationalizations about them and are often better than the rationalizations. Unwise critics often jump—as Matthew Arnold did—to the conclusion that the defining characteristics of the institutionalized great books are the aesthetic and ethical values we derive from them; thus, many plays and poems are stated to be not litera-

Note: This essay was originally published in *Texas Studies in English* 27 (1958): 46–52.

ture at all because the critic does not find the proper values in them. I shall waste no time on such confused and confusing rationalizations but assume instead that more sophisticated critics recognize that formal similarities define *Abie's Irish Rose* as a play and that meter defines the *Ormulum* as poetry. In short, I assume that most serious students of literature recognize that there are both good and bad examples of it and that literary excellence is not the same thing as the defining characteristic of the species. Yet it remains true that the process of definition as described above rests on assumptions which are often tacit and unrecognized and so leave much room for confusion. I have not infrequently met, among students of belles-lettres, the attitude that it is wrong even to attempt the definition of literature. Such students not unnaturally lead the beginner, at least, to believe that unchecked subjectivity is a legitimate method of analysis.

I should propose, therefore, an approach to the problem of definition which closely approximates that of the "great books" criterion yet is different and more consciously held at each step. The procedure rests upon a number of assumptions. First, it is assumed that definition differs from description. Definition should enable the student to recognize all members of the defined class and to exclude all nonmembers of the class; it has no other purpose. Description, on the other hand, should enable the student to recognize all characteristics of all members of the class and should also give him these characteristics in the order of their importance. Definition may make use of quite trivial characteristics and should include no more than what is necessary for discriminatory recognition.

Definition should be based on formal characteristics, since only a formal definition is readily verifiable. Description may and should include many less verifiable matters, even those of values. Definition should, further, precede final description, though this is a statement that needs some elaboration. Obviously the first stage in the process, which leads both to definition and description, is the isolation of a group of items suspected of being or containing a definable class. The characteristics of the group are studied without distinction as to definition and description. Some characteristic or characteristics are selected as possible defining characters and then tested. If, after testing, these prove to be effective discriminators, then the final exhaustive description can begin.

I should propose that the first step is to find a group of utterances parallel to the great books but more inclusive. This group, the corpus, is now fairly widely known and agreed upon. As far as we now know, all communities have produced utterances which they regard sufficiently important so as to be made permanent. These permanent utterances are the corpus for study. A permanent utterance is not necessarily defined as being an example of literature, and occasionally a given utterance, which we might choose to define as literature, will, through accidents of transmission or history, fail of permanent preservation. Yet the corpus can be safely said to contain a sufficient body of examples of literature so that from them we may have some hope of discovering the defining characteristics of literature.

The statement that permanence is not itself a defining characteristic of literature needs emphasis, since it is a point upon which confusion not infrequently arises. If permanence is supposed to be a necessary characteristic of literature, there can then be no contemporary literature, and we should find ourselves in the intolerable position of having to suppose that *Hamlet* was not literature until it had been subjected to a process of aging. On the other hand, however, at least once in my experience I have been able to exclude a given body of utterances from literature because of lack of permanence. In a discussion a colleague and I found ourselves wondering whether the songs that the young unmarried men of the pueblo of Taos sing during courtship were examples of lyric poetry.[1] The songs serve much the same social purposes as lyric poetry in our culture and, therefore, immediately suggest the existence of one of the subtypes of literature. Yet, upon questioning a Taos informant, we discovered that the songs were spontaneous nonsense sequences and spontaneous sequences of notes, identifiable only because they contained the name of a young woman. As a class, they had no permanence at all and could not even be repeated immediately after having been performed. They were not lyric poems and were not literature. It is of some importance to note that this use of permanence as a diagnostic is dependent upon the fact that the whole class of utterances were lacking in permanence. If it were merely a given single utterance which we were thus attempting to exclude, there would be grave danger that lack of permanence was a merely accidental characteristic.

Not only is permanence not a defining characteristic, but it also is itself in need of definition. It is sometimes stated that permanence is essentially a matter of repetitions—that communities insist that certain utterances be repeated from time to time without essential change. To insist upon repetition as the essential form of preservation seems somewhat too narrow. The form of preservation may often enough be memory, capable of preserving an utterance only by repetition; yet, permanence may also take the form of embodying the utterance in some secondary form of symbolism, notably writing. When this happens, permanence need not involve repetition in any ordinary sense. No one, for example, recites all of *Henry Esmond*, even though we do recite lyric poems.

Exactly how much of an utterance is made permanent varies from community to community, and, further, some features of the totality of the communication situation are omitted from preservation in all communities. In permanent utterances in English, for instance, the intonation patterns are very imperfectly given, since the writing system records them only fragmentarily and inaccurately. In some communities, particularly among American Indians, the words, phrases, and even sentences are regarded as outside the permanent recording; so two performers will give, as versions of the same tale, forms which seem to us quite different. A minor by-product of this approach to literature, which sets up the difference between features of the utterance that are a part of the permanent record and those that are excluded, is that it defines the functions of the performer and the area in which he operates. All those parts of the utterance which are outside the permanent record are areas in which the performer is left free choice, and judgments on the comparative excellence of a performance depend upon the choices he makes—they remain quite separate from the parts of the utterance proper. That this by-product is not without value can be seen if one consults the chapter in Wellek and Warren which wrestles manfully but inconclusively with the question of where a poem has its real being.[2]

When a representative corpus of permanent utterances of a given community has been collected, it may then be studied for its linguistic and stylistic characteristics. Within the body of permanent utterances, it is at present a reasonable assumption that there will emerge classes of utterances which differ significantly from casual speech and that in turn there may be other utterances which do not thus differ. Rejection of those utterances which do not differ from casual utterances is an important, even though negative, step in the isolation of literary utterances. A significant objection raised by C. F. Voegelin can be met in this fashion.[3] Voegelin points out that formulas of greeting and departure are essentially permanent, since they are characteristically repeated over and over without essential change. One set of them can be represented by the English expressions *good morning, good afternoon, good night*, and *good-by*. Perhaps the only linguistic item which differs in these utterances from those found in casual forms is the occurrence of an otherwise unidentifiable noun, *by*. Stylistically, the whole set consists of single-construction, or elementless, sentences, and furthermore lacks the permutation characteristics of free constructions—that is, we do not say *bad-by*. It would seem that none of these characteristics are in any way markedly special or different from the characteristics of casual, single-item utterances. Plenty of unique morphemes exist in fixed constructions within casual utterances—Leonard Bloomfield's *cranberry* is the classical example.[4] Also, plenty of unanalyzable single-construction sentences are found in casual language. An example is *attaboy!* Moreover, the analysis of forms like *good-by* shows them to be units quite as much as is a form like *railroad* or *New York*. As I will try to show, literary utterances are essentially characterized by far-reaching relations between items. It is therefore reasonable to say that no utterance that consists of a single item in isolation can be an example of literature. It must be added, however, that what has been done is to exclude English greeting formulas from literature—I should by no means declare that the greeting formulas of other cultures always and necessarily fall outside literature.

It has been said that within the corpus of permanent utterances will be found a class or classes of utterances that differ from casual speech. The differences can be expected to be of two sorts: those that belong to the lower levels of linguistics and those that are stylistic. For these purposes, the lower levels of linguistics consist of those characteristics that can be fully illustrated within the borders of the sentence or of several sentences considered without relation to each other. The inventory of significant sounds is a typical set of such lower-level items, which fall on the level of phonology. Items like stems and endings of words, and words themselves, belong on the level of morphology, and relations between words, as long as they fall within the sentence, belong on the level of syntax.

I have said elsewhere that permanent utterances are characterized by items that may be considered stylistically or are necessarily considered so. The area of stylistics is here defined as that of characteristics and structures that cannot be fully illustrated in a single sentence or in separate sentences considered without relation to each other. The definition is based on the once commonly accepted belief that there is an area of study which describes items within sentences and stops with the border of the sentence. This is the area which I have called the lower levels of linguistics; the area which is not bound by the limits of the sentence is what I have called the area of stylistics.[5] Of course, views of the nature of stylistics differ, and, as I have also said, I do not wish to dogmatize against other views. It is characteristic that items of vocabulary can be studied either in the area of stylistics or on the lower levels of linguistics. If we consider whether the adornment of a woman's head is to be called *hair* or *tresses*, the occurrence of one item or the other within a single sentence is a matter of choice. As a result, some students prefer to describe stylistics as the sum total of choices which the language offers to the individual speaker at each point within the sentence. I think no contradiction exists between the two descriptions—they are complementary. Yet, if we are to describe utterances as wholes, it would seem better to concentrate on relationships that characterize the totality of the utterance, rather than to study only its separate parts. To use the same simple illustration given above, *tresses* and *hair* are choices within the sentence, but, if the rest of the utterance contains sentences like "Her cheeks were like the rose," "Her teeth were like the orient pearl," the occurrence of *tresses* is more probable than *hair*, since *tresses* forms part of a stylistic sequence, each part of which influences the other parts. It is a criticism of much of the study of permanent utterances that it is concerned with the collection of items of vocabulary, individually considered. Far more important would be a study of chains of occurrence, which would be a significant contribution to stylistics. Even with characteristic formulas like the English "Once upon a time there was . . ." stylistic considerations are more important than isolated occurrence. A quite interesting study could be made by tabulating the nouns which occur in, say, the first three sentences of utterances that begin with this sequence.

In short, utterances that are not characterized by stylistic characteristics, which set them off from casual utterances, are not literature. I should submit that those utterances which do thus differ are always examples of literature, at least considered as broadly as possible. A number of cautions are necessary. Obviously, we should not be astonished that many items which pass such a formal stylistic test will turn out to be quite trivial. I should, for instance, have no hesitation in saying that "Thirty days hath September, April, June, and November" is both an example of poetry and a part of English literature. Roman Jakobson has recently pointed out that the intricate assonance and rhyme which link all parts of "I like Ike" are quite sufficient to establish this slogan as a literary text, even if it is not as ancient as "Tippecanoe and Tyler too."[6] Triviality should not alarm us, since the first task is definition, and evaluation should come later.

Second, what would emerge from stylistic study of permanent utterances, at least in most societies, would be several subclasses of utterances, rather than one unified class characterized by a single definable style. These various subclasses will always be easier to isolate and define than are the larger and more inclusive groupings. In practice, we recognize this. We characteristically have no difficulty in recognizing a sonnet since we do it formally by recognizing the rhyme scheme and meter. We have more difficulty in recognizing an inclusive class like poetry and more and more difficulty as we add other classes like novels. A reasonable procedure, I should suggest, is to start with those subclasses that are clearly marked by definable stylistic characteristics, to exhaust these characteristics, and then to use them for the definition of other subclasses of literature until we have finally arrived at a complete formulation of the classes and subclasses of stylistically marked permanent utterances for each community under study.

To give an example of the kind of difficulty that can be anticipated and the type of solution that can at least be hoped for, we can consider such things as ritual and law. Both produce texts that are characteristically permanent, and both have stylistic characteristics that should eventually be definable. Legal style, for instance, notably contains items like *whereas* and *party of the first part* linked in chains of occurrence. English ritual, or at least some kinds of ritual, contain linked items like *thou*, *thee*, and verb endings of *-eth*. Such a mere sampling is not accurate enough to define either ritualistic or legal style but should be enough to suggest an approach for a more thorough study. When the style of each type of utterance has been sufficiently studied so as to define each with precision, it should only then be profitable to study the various social conditions under which each is produced, the social values each serves, and the social occasions at which each is invoked and repeated. Such final study and description should then enable us to settle the status of each type, enabling us to say definitely that ritual is a subtype of literature either better included in or better excluded from some such narrower class as belles-lettres.

The burden of this essay has been to insist that literature has its being in the area of stylistics and that definition of literature must be sought in stylistics. It is, I further believe, not merely true that stylistic characteristics are the defining marks of literature but also true that close and exhaustive study of stylistics is our best hope of learning to understand the total qualities of literature. I am not saying that the values in literature are unimportant—I am, rather, saying that as analytical students it behooves us to be sure that we have exhausted stylistic matters before we begin a rigorous analysis of values. Such a study, I can assure you, from having made a few attempts in a simple sphere—that of lyric poetry—is as yet in its infancy. At present, it requires great labor merely to isolate and describe the stylistic items and relationships of a short utterance like a triolet. We have not yet begun to formulate an attack on the extremely long-span relationships that characterize novels.

Chapter Two
Toward a Literary Analysis

The clearest statement of the value that our society places on literature is the following pair of sentences from Matthew Arnold: "More and more mankind will discover that we have to turn to poetry to interpret life for us, to console us, to sustain us. Without poetry, our science will appear incomplete; and most of what now passes with us for religion and philosophy will be replaced by poetry."[1] Under such a view of the nature of literature the function of the critic is plain. He finds the spiritual values that the poet has created, expounds them, and passes them on to readers who might not find them for themselves. Indeed, as Arnold's own criticism showed, the critic is only a subtype of the poet, no less concerned with the interpretation of life than the poet himself. This is a high view of the function of the critic, and a criticism which follows such a program will always enjoy a place of honor. I believe that it is a fair statement that our current criticism follows this program, sometimes successfully and nobly, sometimes imperfectly and unimaginatively, but always with fidelity and conviction.

Yet this program has not resulted in unmixed good. There have been many attempts to develop a different and more scientific approach to the study of literature—attempts which have rather generally met with denunciation, even when they have been tactfully and tentatively advanced. It must be admitted, however, that many of the attempts have been characterized by an irrelevance and even a naïveté that would seem to prove the denunciators right. The irrelevance has been shown by those academicians who have avoided the investigation of literature in favor of the more comfortably factual fields of dates, sources, and biography. The naïveté has been shown by those who have tried to transfer the measuring techniques of the exact sciences to literature, without allowance for the quality of the unique material to be measured. Yet it will, I think, be generally admitted that the defects of scientists ought not to be used to condemn science. It seems to me that those who have attempted to set up an analysis of literature have failed, not because the attempt is impossible, but because they have not been sufficiently aware that the discipline

Note: This essay was originally published in *Studies in Honor of James Southall Wilson*, ed. Fredson Bowers, University of Virginia Studies, vol. 4 (Charlottesville: University of Virginia Press, 1951), pp. 280–285.

they were striving for was different from anything that goes under the name of criticism. The axioms on which such a study should be based are different, as are the conclusions that it could be expected to reach. Further, by definition as a different study, it ought to be clear that it is not much more or not much less antagonistic to traditional forms of literary study than dancing, say, is to trout fishing. The same man can carry on both activities; disaster will result only if he tries to carry them both on at the same time. I shall attempt to give some programmatic statements about an analytic study of literature, some of which, it is hoped, may be useful to critics, at least when they are dealing with the facts rather than the values of literature. I shall at the end of this essay give a very small specimen of literary analysis, which I have tried to make more sophisticated, more relevant, and more rigorous in method than some previous attempts. Neither the general statements nor the specimen of analysis should be construed as an attack on the position that literature and criticism are interpretations of life. I am making a plea for tolerance of a type of study that has not yet been extensively tried.

Both the background knowledge for literary analysis and the techniques by which it should be carried out come from the science of language. Such a statement may seem extravagant since, in spite of the fact that linguistics and literature have had a sort of uneasy marriage for two generations, it is a common attitude that linguistics is a narrow specialty having little to do with all that makes literature worth studying. Typical is the attitude of Cleanth Brooks that linguistics achieves a utility, which it would not otherwise possess, when it is used to furnish the critic with the detailed information without which he could not operate, but which only the critic knows how to use most worthily. Linguists themselves, indeed, have contributed to this view of their activity as remote and bloodless. Most of us can remember classes in older literature where we were prevented from getting at the literature by the necessity of studying details of the history of inflections. The history of inflections is a fascinating study when carried on in its proper sphere, but I think that most modern linguists would be prepared to admit that the poetry of Chaucer can be fully appreciated without knowing that *ete* 'eat' is a fifth-class strong verb, that it shows the same grade of ablaut in the Latin and Germanic past tense plurals, and that these plurals once contained an Indo-European laryngeal. Linguistic history is indeed a relatively narrow specialty, just as is the history of chemistry. But nowadays neither linguistics nor chemistry is an essentially historical discipline.

A broader view of linguistics would define it as that branch of cultural anthropology which deals with the nature and structure of the most basic and complete form of symbolic activity—the noises we make with our faces.

Speech not only is that activity which is most characteristically human—far more so than cooking, wearing clothes, and making war—it also is that activity without which all other forms of organized human activity would be impossible. A given individual may, it is true, drive a car or build a house even though deprived of speech, but no such activity would be open to him were he not a member of a society that has developed these activities by means of language. Speech, in short, is what most fully distinguishes us from the other animals, and the science that studies it is basically important to an understanding of the human world.

Perhaps the best summation of the current status of linguistics as a science has been made by Martin Joos:

> . . . within our field we must adopt a technique of precise treatment, which is by definition a mathematics. We must make our "linguistics" a kind of mathematics within which inconsistency is by definition impossible . . . Have linguists succeeded in setting up such a mathematical style for describing language? Well, not quite; but our science is still young. In its mathematical phase it is just a quarter of a century old, for we date it from Bloomfield's "Set of Postulates for the Science of Language," (in the journal *Language* in 1925). And even physics has not yet entirely resolved the conflict between quantum theory and the wave theory of light. But of all the sciences and near-sciences which deal with human behavior, linguistics is the only one which is in a fair way to becoming completely mathematical, and other social sciences are already beginning to imitate the strict methods of the linguists.[2]

This newer, stricter, and more descriptive linguistics is not yet known everywhere, since many leading scholars received their language training before the full impact of Bloomfieldian linguistics and, consequently, think of language study as still rightly Grimm's law, Gothic, and the grades of ablaut. The newer linguistics takes as its aim not merely the reconstruction of ancestral forms but the complete understanding of language activity, in both its structure and its content. We can, in spite of difficulties in the way, hope that eventually we will be able to demonstrate the correspondences between the structure of language activity and the structure of all other organized human activities; in short, we can hope that semantics (with a small *s*, be it noted) may someday become a part both of science and of linguistics. It must, however, be frankly admitted that semantics is as yet by no means within the linguist's grasp—we often find ourselves wishing for a language comfortably without meaning, just as the analytical bibliographer often wishes for books without words. Yet it is also fair to point out that the recent work of such linguists as George L. Trager, Murray Emeneau, and Harry Hoijer holds out some hope for the investigation of structural parallels between language and culture, which may eventually give us a means of making statements about semantics that are both systematic and verifiable.

This brief discussion of linguistics is meant to justify the position that linguistics is a broad and important kind of investigation—broad enough and important enough to be not only a way of investigating casual speech but also a way of investigating literature. In fact, linguists would now say that language occurs in acts called utterances and that literary works are a subclass of utterances. Of course, to make such a statement understandable, I must immediately add that literary works are often, indeed nowadays usually, utterances in writing rather than in audible speech. It is not my intention here to go into the relation of speech and writing, but a brief statement may be helpful. Writing is a substitute for speech, interchangeable with it, as a stimulus for the hearer's or reader's internal, silent but still linguistic, response. From another point of view, writing is the author's substitute embodiment of his internal language in letters rather than in sounds. If a literary work is then a subclass of linguistic utterances, it would seem that the relevance of linguistics to literature is fully established.

The question of where a work of literature has its real existence is then no more difficult of solution than the same question concerning any utterance in any language. I shall not take it up in detail here; I shall simply say that if acts of language have some sort of existence in the outside world, then works of literature also have such an external locus.

The position just taken throws into sharp focus a basic difference between a critical and an analytic approach to literature. Critics often say that the poem exists in the mind of the reader, in the mind of the right reader, in a sort of union between the mind of the right reader and the mind of the author, or even, as in Wellek and Warren, in the collective minds of successive ages of right readers. In fact, it would be quite possible for a sufficiently idealistic critic to come to the conclusion that the poem exists in some ideal form quite outside human experience. All of these positions offer difficulty, for if the worth of the poem lies in an individual reaction, or in an unknowable realm, it would seem that all literary evaluation is reduced to confusion. Yet, for the critic, the confusion is more apparent than real since the difficulty is a logical one, and criticism by definition transcends logic. In short, the critic evaluates by reference to emotional and spiritual values, which for the critic, poet, and even scientist are admitted to be the deepest and most satisfying part of human experience. It comes therefore as a shock to find that the analyst cannot work with these assumptions when he approaches literature. If the poem exists in the reader's head or if it exists in an unreachable ideal, it is beyond investigation. If the poem is beyond investigation, the analyst, in turn, can make no statements at all about it. I ask the reader, then, not to deny the reality of the reader's reaction to the poem and not to deny the intangible values of literature but to grant the possibility of a heuristic assumption in the hope that greater understanding may come from it. The assumption is that a piece of literature has reality in the outside world as a linguistic act. It can then be investigated like any other linguistic act and can be assumed to have characteristics of its own, which exist whether or not they have been analyzed. The situation is closely paralleled in the history of linguistics, which, as I have said, investigates utterances, though of a less-special sort than the utterances that make up literature. It is obvious that a part of language exists inside the heads of the hearer and speaker, and many linguists today feel that this internal part of language is the most important portion of it. Some even go as far as to condemn much of the linguistics of the forties and fifties merely because the internal components of language necessarily escape the analysis of overt utterances.[3] But to insist that it is no use to investigate linguistics behavioristically because overt behavior is not the whole of language is to keep linguistics in a prescientific stage and to deny the tremendous advance made by Leonard Bloomfield and his followers.[4]

Granted the assumption that a piece of literature exists in the outside world as a linguistic act, it follows that the investigator of literature needs to know about language—the larger whole of which literature forms a part. Put analogically, the analyst of literature who has no knowledge of language structure is like an analyst of the sonnet who does not know that sonnets are only one type of English poetry. Students of literature are wary of making statements of fact that are in conflict with the results of analytical bibliography; they are curiously less wary of making statements characterized by the errors of the linguistic layman, even though such statements may vitiate all conclusions based upon them. For instance, critics, who should know better, all too often confuse letters and sounds. Not infrequently I have found myself explaining to students of literature, supposedly past the training level, that no assonance occurs in some such line as "The lonely dove moves not with mothlike wing." Often enough someone will make the puzzled comment "Why not? They're all *o*'s aren't they?"

Again, I have heard a critic of international prestige make the statement that the Milton line "whilst the Lantskip round it measures" contains a vowel harmony that is destroyed by modernization to "landscape." The difficulty with such a statement is that it is not realized that before vowel harmony can be proved to be characteristic of an utterance, the harmony must be shown to be present in a degree greater than would be found in a random arrangement. Differences in dialects and in systems of analysis occur, but the syllabics of English are at most not many more than twenty and, in some systems, rather less. There are twenty syllables in a pentameter couplet. Even if the poet makes a determined effort to differentiate, there will be repetitions. Vowel harmony, however, is supposed to include not merely identical vowels but vowels that are of the same order—back vowels, perhaps, in contrast to front vowels. It seems evident, then, that harmony can be demonstrated only if all the vowels are of one order or if the sequence is shown to be fixed by occurring more than once. Otherwise, any arrangement at all—the nonsense line that I quoted above,

> The lonely dove moves not with mothlike wing,
> /ow/   /ə/   /uw/   /a/   /ɔ/

with the variety of stressed vowels all spelled with the letter *o*—could be stated to be a subtle example of vowel harmony without fear of contradiction.

More important, and less frequently realized, is the fact that a great deal in the external form of literature, whether prose or poetry, is dependent on the structure of the language in which it is written and cannot be understood without a knowledge of that structure. It is not, for instance, an accident that Japanese poetry lacks rhyme. In a language that permits only a very small number of sounds in the final position in phrase and sentence, rhyme occurs everywhere and cannot be used as an added ornament. The patterned arrangement of pitches that characterizes one type of Chinese poetry is possible only in a language that uses pitch differences to distinguish words. It is impossible in a language like English, which uses pitch differences only to distinguish sentences. In English prose and poetry, alliteration is regarded as an ornament, while I am told that a careful French stylist corrects it away if it happens to occur. Alliteration can be used as a stylistic effect in English by making it coincide with recurrent strongly stressed syllables preceded by a pause that is at least minimal. Since French lacks the stress and pause patterns of contrast found in English, alliteration becomes merely pointless repetition. Similarly, a writer of English prose who allowed such elements as *-ation*, *-icity*, or the like to pile up through the course of a paragraph would be felt to have produced intolerable cacophony. Such Latin endings as *-arum* and *-ibus*, on the other hand, are a necessary part of the structure of concord in that language. Not only is it true that Latin cannot be written without their frequent recurrence, but also some evidence even suggests that Latin readers took pleasure in them. At least Ciceronian Latin departs from the order of speech as we see it reflected in Vulgar Latin to give the well-known rooflike sentence arrangement which has the effect of scattering repetitions at symmetrical points throughout the utterance. A final example will bring the principle closer to home. Chaucer's verse has syllabic regularity, often secured by padding words, which would be the mark of an unskillful poet were he writing today. Middle English had many terminations that could be treated as syllabic or not, according to sentence conditions. Further, there were many vocalic endings which, without much regard to spelling and etymology, were pronounced or not in the same way. Middle English had, therefore, an enormous amount of syllabic leeway absent in Modern English, which invited regularity of verse structure. To criticize Chaucer because he does not follow modern conventions is merely to say that he does not write Modern English.

The consideration of the relation of literary form to language structure brings me to a more general statement, which is one that must be faced by critic and analyst alike. I have said that criticism owes much to Matthew Arnold. Arnold many times stated that he was trying to set up, not a relative and historical standard of criticism, but an absolute and universal one.[5] It is just this attempt that, to a linguist, seems so premature as to be an error. If literature is admitted to be a part of culture, it follows that literary form, literary content, and literary standards necessarily differ from place to place and time to time, just as cultures have been abundantly proved to differ from place to place and time to time. Only when the differences have been thoroughly studied—as it seems to me they have not—can the necessarily few and generalized universals be distilled out of them. An attempt to write a universal literary aesthetics without such study seems as naïve as the supposed early attempts to write a universal grammar by giving the Finnish or Chinese equivalents of the Latin ablative absolute. Even comparative literature seems to me to lack much of the broadness of base necessary for generalization about universals. As far as I know comparative literature, it seems to concern itself largely with such matters as the study of the versions of the Don Juan story in Spain, Germany, and England. Such a study is, of course, worthwhile, but it leaves the larger aim untouched. A comparative study is needed that attacks such questions as what things in language and culture account for the fact that Japanese write haiku while we write limericks. Or, further, Why is Africa the homeland of the proverb; India, the homeland of the animal fable?

Such broad studies may seem far from home, but the attitude they would foster is badly needed by both critic and teacher. The absolutist critic often enough commits absurdities, even within the framework of relatively modern English literature. For instance, I recently heard one of our most respected dramatic critics maintain that *The Duchess of Malfi* is a bad play because in form and content it is unsuited for production on the Broadway stage. Literary criticism could profit—as some critics have seen—by the relativism that characterizes much of linguistics.[6] It seems possible to me that the disturbing survey that recently showed every classic had earned a considerable degree of active student dislike may indicate that teachers have been trying to make students like *Tom Jones* as directly and naturally as they like a poem by Allen Ginsberg. If the teacher is unwilling or unable to explain the differences in form and content between the works of the present and the past, the student will inevitably assume that past art is a merely stuffy and inferior attempt at present art.

As well as greater relativism, the analysis of literature needs greater consistency. The absence of consistency is a fault conspicuous in the writings of the New Critics, who seem so sure that they are both different and wonderfully sought after. It is impossible not to sympathize with their insistence that statements about a work of literature necessitate examination of it and their further insistence that what is said about a work of literature must be relevant. At the same time, their rejection of historical studies has given them a special contempt for consistency of method that makes them often as bad as the antiquarians they are attacking. For instance, Cleanth Brooks defends the colorlessness of the personifications in Thomas Gray's *Elegy* on the ground that they were made as dull and empty as possible in order to contrast with the more concrete portions of the poem which constitute its chief virtue.[7] Such a statement might be consistent with the relative attitude described above, but it is not so presented. That is, Brooks assumes that an empty use of personifications is a blemish even in terms of eighteenth-century conventions. Yet, having made this assumption, he finds a way to praise the poem for qualities he has assumed are defects. The praise reduces all else that Brooks has said about the poem to contradiction. In short, no one, critic or analyst, can assume that whiteness is a universal virtue and then praise something because it is black.

To pass to more specific considerations of literary analysis, we must leave such general suggestions about point of view and method as have just been given and consider content, since it is a truism that no study of literature is worth anything unless it gives even more attention to content than to form. I have said that linguistics has as yet very imperfect control over matters of meaning so that it might seem that linguistics, contrary to what was earlier asserted, could have nothing to say of literary content. Indeed, if linguistics should remain content with studying form alone, the objection would be valid. The linguist's problem—to quote students of phonemics—is that the symbols of language are arranged in systems, the parts of which are discrete, while the experience signified by language seems to be arranged in continuity.[8] The linguist must then shove continuity clear out of his field of inquiry or somehow translate it into discreteness. Stated in this way, the conflict between criticism and linguistics is not so very important; the critic has to make a transition like the linguist's from the continuity of experience to the discrete words and phrases in which these experiences are recorded in literature.

Linguistics has had conspicuous success of late in translating continuity into discreteness, not in the sphere of semantics, but in the sphere of language sounds. Language sounds exist on two levels: one as physical and articulatory entities where they are mere noises and one on a linguistic level as functioning signals. On the physical level they share the continuity of all that is outside language—that is, considered as mere noises, it is impossible to say that the initial and medial sounds of *totter* are more like each other than either is to the initial and medial sounds of *dodder*. No sharp physical dividing line exists. Faced with this problem, the linguist follows a method of approximation well known in science. Following common sense and intuition, he makes a series of initial cuts, separating sounds into like and unlike. His procedure endeavors to avoid gross error, but it is tentative and probably logically indefensible. When the cuts have been made, however, it turns out that the intuitively chosen entities arrange themselves into a symmetrical pattern, a sort of system of intersecting lines as when we say that labial quality occurs in the English sounds [b p m], dental quality in [d t n], stop quality in [b p d t], voice in [b m d n], and so on. It turns out, further, to be possible to judge the rightness of the cuts by the symmetry, economy, and completeness of the structuralized pattern that results. For instance, some English sounds are characterized by aspiration; others are not. Yet, since no structuralized statement of English sounds can be made on the basis of aspiration without loss in symmetry and economy, the linguist feels justified in disregarding aspiration in his cuts. He has, then, reduced the continuity of noise to discrete language symbols, often called phonemes, and has tested his results by the structure they give him. He need no longer worry over the unlikeness of the consonants of *totter*; in English they belong to the same phoneme.[9]

A number of attempts, as yet hesitant though forward-looking, have recently been made within linguistics to apply this same structural method to identification of semantic entities. Of these, the one to which my own essay owes most is an investigation by Professor Zellig Harris.[10] I have said that literature is a type of utterance characterized by heightened symmetry of structure. It therefore offers a particularly fruitful field for the discovery of patterning, and the linguistic analysis of literature can now be defined. It consists in a tentative identification of units of meaning within a literary utterance and then the testing of this identification by the structuralized statement that results from it. The procedure—though not the materials analyzed—will be similar to the analysis of language sounds.

On the lowest level, the data are the words and word elements, together with their meanings, found in the poem—in linguistic terms, the morphemes and sememes. The data on this level are incapable of exact definition. These units will then be organized into relatively abstractly stated minor utterances or sentences. From the minor utterances it is hoped that a structure will emerge that can then be taken as a statement of the meaning of the poem as a whole. The final statement is parallel to the linguist's final statement of the sound-structure of the language he is analyzing. The units of meaning that will be set up are not to be thought of as having universal application; they are valid for this utterance alone. They are not, in short, like dictionary definitions; they are more nearly akin to the figures and images which are the traditional tools of criticism. They differ from figures and images in that they are not mentalistic units and consequently escape the fatal difficulty in using images as analytic tools—that of knowing whether a given word contains a mental picture or is used merely as a part of some unanalyzed total formula.

The poem that I have chosen as a suitable problem for analysis is the song which accompanies Bassanio's choice:

> *Tell me where is fancie bred,*
> *Or in the heart, or in the head:*
> *How begot, how nourished. Replie, replie.*
> *It is engendred in the eyes,*
> *With gazing fed, and Fancie dies,*
> *In the cradle where it lies:*
> *Let us all ring Fancies knell.*
> Ile begin it.
> *Ding, dong, bell.*
> All. *Ding, dong, bell.*[11]

I have admitted that my raw data are impossible to define exactly. I must work with these raw data on the level of common sense and intuition but will endeavor to keep my definitions as free as possible from obvious error. Clearly a first necessary step is to consult previous scholars to be sure that I do not miss necessary background knowledge. The previous scholarship is not very helpful for my problem. One group of articles attempts to find a source for the poem, immediate or remote.[12] Probably the chief value of these articles is to demonstrate that the poem belongs to a well-marked type of love poetry in which the entry of love through the eye is a commonplace. A second group of comments tries to demonstrate that the poem is a hint to direct Bassanio's choice.[13] These comments can be disregarded, since we will be primarily concerned with the poem as a unity in itself, rather than as a part of the play as a whole. A few scholars have concerned themselves with whether the poem was sung as a duet or a solo.[14] These analyses also can be disregarded since the question is one of playhouse representation rather than structure. It will emerge that sound structural evidence suggests that the poem concerns itself with two figures: man and woman. Only one article is genuinely helpful: Charles Read Baskervill's excellent study, "Bassanio as an Ideal Lover."[15] Baskervill lays the necessary groundwork by pointing out that the poem is part of Elizabethan love lore and must be understood in the light of a set of conventions we no longer share. This love lore was the result of a blend between Renaissance Neoplatonism and medieval courtly love and held that "fancie," the first stage of love, led through a series of rigidly defined steps of abstraction and a search for ever more idealized beauty to a final contemplation of the beauty of God. All this, of course, is familiar to any reader of Spenser's *Fowre Hymnes*. It is, however, a cogent example of the necessary relativism, since these ideas once taken so seriously could hardly be expected to be immediately intelligible to a student in a contemporary literature class.

We are now ready to begin some tentative identifications. Clearly one of the important words in the poem is "fancie," which Baskervill tells us should be read not in any modern meaning but as the beginning of love. "Fancie" is identified throughout as an infant, which is born and can die. One reason for this identification is that "fancie" is simply the first stage of something. A second obvious reason is that in European literature love itself is identified with the infant Cupid. A third reason for the identification has been overlooked by scholars, though the fact is well known. In Elizabethan English one meaning of the word *baby* is "image reflected in the pupil of the eye." The meaning occurs in the fairly common phrase "looking babies" said of lovers at gaze.[16] From this general background there emerges, then, one of the basic symbolic units of the poem, namely, "baby." Curiously enough, man and woman, or lover and mistress, are nowhere overtly mentioned in the poem, any more than "image in the eye." However, I believe that, if "baby" is taken as one of the basic units, it is reasonable to suppose that the presence of it in a love poem clearly implies the presence of the man and woman who are the lovers and the potential parents. I shall therefore make the assumption that the three basic symbolic units are "man," "woman," and "baby." These I shall arrange in the abstract sentence "man plus woman gives birth of baby" and its negative "man minus woman gives death of baby."

I am now ready, having developed my minor sentences, to see what structure emerges from them. The formulas I have given above are in themselves a pair of semantic triads but are in dualistic opposition. The triadic nature of the formulas is shown in that each unit of the poem consists of three minor units, senses, or meanings. The man of the poem can be the male singer, all male lovers, or Bassanio. Similarly, the woman can be the female singer, all female lovers, or Portia. The baby is the image in the eye, infant love, and a human child. These separate symbolic meanings give, in turn, three interpretations of both the positive and negative formulas. In the positive formula, the first level is that, as the male singer looks at the female singer, there will be a reflection in her eye; the second is that, as man is attracted by woman, love is born; the third is that, if Bassanio and Portia are married, a child will be conceived. In the negative formula, if the singer turns away, the reflection will disappear; if lovers prove unworthy, love will die; if Bassanio and Portia do not marry, their unborn child will die. The final, and in some sense the deepest, symbolic level in the poem represents a return to dualistic form, which thus can be said to close the structure. This final dualism can be stated in the paradoxical form: death of baby equals birth of baby. That is, at each level the loss of something lower is replaced by the gain of something higher. The eye image is replaced by love; love is replaced by marriage; and even the possible loss of this marriage is equated with the possible gain of completely spiritualized love.

I have two things to say about this structure before I pass to a conclusion. First, like any statement of pattern, it is capable of being represented by an abstract spatial diagram, though I will spare my readers the algebraic arrangement of formulas, which they can readily construct for themselves. Second, complete and perfect symmetry seems never to characterize language activity. For instance, no matter how presented, the English sound /t/ is not in perfect alignment with such other English sounds as /p/ and /k/. A residue of data that does not fit the pattern without some hacking is always evident. Such minor imperfections are not taken as proof of invalidity; instead it is assumed that that structure is nearest the truth which has the fewest of them. The most important residue in the structure I have presented seems to concern the human infant. It is not literally true that a human child dies if its parents are parted, in the same sense that the eye image disappears if the gazer looks away.

The analysis and structure which I have presented—in full knowledge that many would deny the relevance of scientific procedures in literature—are intended as a tiny piece of descriptive science. Working within the scientific frame, I have been prevented from taking into account any emotional values which may be found in the poem, though I say again that I am not denying their existence. Also, I have not intended the analysis to be a demonstration of the worth of the poem, though I believe it is a reasonable assumption that many pieces of writing generally agreed to be inferior would not reveal the tightness of structure found here. Most emphatically I must disclaim the idea that this particular type of structure demonstrates superiority.[17] Any such generalization would be premature and must await the analysis of more literary material.

I am aware that differing standards for judgment of my analysis will be applied by those of my readers who are critics and by those who are linguists. The critic will judge the usefulness of the analysis by whether it increases his pleasure in the poem. To the critic I may then be allowed to observe that traditional methods are not fully successful with this poem. If we judge the poem as the statement of a profound truth, the poem seems commonplace. If we judge it imagistically, it turns out to be a sort of monstrous mixed metaphor.

As a linguist, however, I should wish my analysis to be judged by the criteria that are universal in logical description of data. If my statement of pattern brings out unity in the poem by subsuming all its symbolism under a single plan characterized by statable relationships between each part and each other part, it is symmetrical; if it does not leave out any symbolic elements, it is complete; if it does not contradict itself at any point, it is consistent. Again, even if it fulfills these requirements, it is like all other scientific statements in that it is not uniquely true but is a hypothesis to be accepted only until it is replaced by a better hypothesis. This final statement constitutes the only answer to an objection that I am sure will appear. Critics unfamiliar with the nature of scientific hypotheses may say that this analysis is ingenious but that some other analysis might be equally possible. I can only say that I would welcome any analysis that turned out to be better. In the meantime, I have tested my own analysis by trying all the alternatives I can think of.

The value of this essay for linguists should be clear. I have tried to make use of structural characteristics as a means of research in the field of meaning and hope that the grammar I have written for a single poem will suggest the possibility of writing similar grammars for other literary utterances. To those of my readers who are critics, I can conclude by reiterating a plea for understanding and tolerance. Analysis of literature that is concerned with patterns and is linguistically based is as yet a largely untried method of study, and it is therefore too soon to evaluate it. At least it looks promising enough to be pursued further. Information about literature is both scarce and valuable; thus, no promising technique should be neglected. Only when a technique has been thoroughly tried will there be any need to decide whether it is more or less valuable than other techniques. In the meantime, both analyst and critic can well work side by side in the hope that each may increase the sum total of understanding of problems which often overlap.

Chapter Three
Pippa's Song:
Two Attempts
at Structural Criticism

> *The year's at the spring*
> *And day's at the morn;*
> *Morning's at seven;*
> *The hill-side's dew-pearled;*
> *The lark's on the wing;*
> *The snail's on the thorn:*
> *God's in his heaven–*
> *All's right with the world!*
>   ROBERT BROWNING

John Crowe Ransom, in an able and important critical study, recently re-marked of *Pippa's Song* that its last two lines were "a tag of identification so pointed as to be embarrassing." Thereafter he went on to justify the state-ment: "She spends three lines dating the occasion very precisely . . . . Then come three details which constitute the concrete: the hillside, the lark, the snail . . . . And that would be the poem; except that she must conclude by putting in her theological Universal."[1]

Ransom's approach is in terms of pattern. He sees in the poem an arrange-ment of two three-line groups followed by a two-line conclusion. He con-demns the conclusion because it does not seem to be properly related to the preceding material. It would appear that the units with which he has operated are essentially semantic: units of time, units of concrete experience, and a unit of abstract theological universality. If the operating units are valid, his state-ment of the structure and the resultant evaluation follow almost inevitably.

His units are not, however, the only ones that might be chosen. In metrical structure the poem is remarkably rigid, each line being ended by a terminal juncture, with no terminal junctures within the lines. Each juncture group has the grammatical form of a sentence, with subject, verb, and complement. The lines of the poem therefore invite the interpretation that they are the normal first segments, since they are defined as units by their formal and grammatical structure. Even at this stage, divergence from Ransom's segmentation results.

Note: This essay was originally published in *Texas Studies in English* 35 (1956): 51–56.

Ransom has taken the last two lines as one unit, not two, because both are concerned with the "theological Universal." To group them thus, he must disregard the linguistic characteristics which mark line 8 as separate from line 7.

Yet, the eight separate lines cannot be presumed to be unrelated. A second task is, therefore, to search for and describe this relationship since, if the poem has a general pattern, it must reside in its parts and their relationships to each other and to the whole. Because the parts are sentences, the relationships between them belong to the study of stylistics (which deals with relationships between sentences) rather than linguistics (which deals with relationships within sentences). Typical stylistic relationships show themselves in the repetition of formal patterns from one sentence to the next.

The first three lines have the grammatical structure of noun, copula, and prepositional phrase headed by a noun. Line 4, on the other hand, has the structure of noun, copula, and phrasal modifier. Lines 5, 6, and 7 repeat the structure of the first three lines. Line 8 has the structure found in line 4: noun, copula, and modifying phrase. For this reason, lines 1, 2, and 3 show formal similarity to lines 5, 6, and 7, and line 4 also shows formal similarity to line 8. In form, then, line 8 is related to line 4 rather than primarily to line 7 as Ransom stated. The formal similarity between lines 4 and 8 is backed by their linkage in rhyme.

The relationships so far stated have been arrived at by study of formal characteristics. Such a procedure is similar to that of linguistic analysis. It is true that the subject of analysis is here a printed text, in contrast to the oral material with which linguistics habitually operates. The difference is more apparent than real. Browning's punctuation, like that of English written composition generally, does not give a clear picture of the phonological structure. In analysis of any printed text it is necessary to read it aloud so that thereafter it can be treated as a spoken utterance. The reading given to the poem is not to be defended as the necessarily right interpretation. It has been checked with several other speakers of English and can, therefore, be described as a natural and possible rendering however it may differ in detail from others.

If formal characteristics have been exhausted, the next step is consideration of lexical meanings. The content of line 1, "The year's at the spring," can be stated in general terms. *Year* is a large unit of time, and *spring* is a unit contained within it. Many readers would agree that, in human terms, *spring* is the best of the contained units. The statement that *spring* is the best unit within the year is not forced by the structure of this line. It is a hypothesis to be tested by its results in analysis of the rest of the poem.

Line 2, "And day's at the morn," also contains a larger unit of time and a contained unit, though the larger unit of this line is smaller than the larger unit of the first line. When sentences are stylistically linked by structure, it is to be expected that there will be analogies in meaning as well. If the hypothesis about line 1 is correct, it is reasonable to suppose that *morn* is also the best of the contained entities.

In line 3, "Morning's at seven," there is once more a larger unit of time and a contained unit. By stylistic implication, the contained unit is again the best of its group. Moreover, an additional fact emerges from line 3. *Morning* is a form exchangeable with *morn*, so that the contained unit of line 2 is the containing unit of line 3. In stylistic relations, particularly those in the relatively permanent form of literature, spans of interpretation can spread backward as well as forward, and it is, therefore, possible to reinterpret the relationships in the earlier lines. The entities in the first three lines descend in a general order from larger to smaller. Yet it is possible that the pattern is even more precisely parallel and that *spring* and *day* are in the same relationship to each other as *morn* and *morning*. The point cannot be settled, since it is obvious that *spring* and *day* are not exchangeable, but the suggestion is certainly there. A reasonable reading might, therefore, assume that the structure of the poem has equated the two words. The first three lines can now be given in a schematic statement of the stylistic structure, which emerges from lexical examination:

Large A is at contained B (its best)
Smaller B is at contained C (its best)
Still smaller C is at contained D (its best).

In the grammatically different line 4, "The hill-side's dew-pearled," *hill-side* can be defined as a part of the physical scene. In contrast to a unit like *world* in line 8, it is a small and immediate part. The phrasal modifier, *dew-pearled*, indicates a state in which the hillside is certainly attractive. A generalized statement is "little X is good Y." Line 4, though related to line 8, is also related to the lines that precede. Carrying forward the hypothesis that the contained units are the best of the several groups, one can see in the attractive state of the hillside a similar excellence: being dew-pearled is its best state. The formulaic statement should, therefore, be revised to "little X is good Y (its best)." Further relationships between the first three lines and line 4 are not explicitly indicated, but, as stated earlier, a change in grammatical form and content takes place with line 4. The tightly knit sequence of the first three lines is broken by a statement of a different sort, though one which is related to the preceding lines. In linguistic analysis, as in the everyday interpretation of speech, it is a sensible procedure to settle on the interpretation of highest probability and to disregard all others. There is no reason why this technique should not be used here. The most probable interpretation of the meaning of such an incremental change is that the relationship is one of cause and result. *Post hoc, ergo propter hoc* may not be good logic, but it is good probabilistic interpretation of stylistic sequences. A final statement of line 4 is, then, "therefore small X is Y (its best)."

Now that the lexical and stylistic pattern has been tentatively established, the rest of the poem can be more quickly described. Lines 5, 6, and 7 move, in general, from small objects to large. The objects are living beings, and the prepositional phrases which follow the copulas are, by analogy from the content of the first four lines, the proper and best place for each of these beings. It is true that *wing* is not strictly a place in the same sense as *thorn* or *heaven*, but the minor difference is overridden by stylistic similarity to the surrounding sentences. The order from small to large is a reversal of the order in the first group of lines. Yet, this ascending order is itself reversed by lines 5 and 6, where *snail* is smaller than *lark*. The break has a startling result in that it brings the extremes of the scale, *snail* and *God*, into immediate juxtaposition. We can therefore represent lines 5, 6, and 7 thus:

> Small E is on F (its best place)
> Smaller G is on H (its best place)
> Large I is in J (its best place).

Line 8 is also readily describable. It, like line 4, is a result—"therefore the large scene is at its best." The statement that the poem deals with best entities and states has, up to this point, been a hypothesis—not contradicted at any point, but without confirmation. The last line furnishes explicit confirmation in the words "all's right." A final statement of the pattern of the poem is now: three analogically related descending statements and their results on a small scale, then three analogically related ascending statements and their results on a large scale. The surprise in structure is the departure from order, which brings the smallest and largest entities of the second part into contiguity.

The analysis of this poem has been thus labored only partly because of a desire to arrive at an interpretation and not at all because of a fondness for elaboration. The attempt has been to work out an orderly critical procedure having a maximum of rigor at each step. The method should therefore be defined. It might at first sight seem to be linguistic, since linguistic data have been used at a number of points. Such a description would not be accurate. The method falls wholly beyond the upper level of linguistics, that is, in those portions of the communication situation beyond the fields of phonology, morphology, and syntax. The linguistic data (phonology and grammar) were used as a tool for the first segmentation of the poem into constituents in a fashion similar to the use of phonetic data for a preliminary segmenting of the sounds of speech into phonemic units.

I have taken up a detailed description of the levels of literary analysis and statement elsewhere.[2] Here, it is sufficient to say that the preliminary units of literary analysis are below the threshold of literary structure and study, just as the phonetic characteristics of speech are below the threshold of linguistic structure and statement. The parallel between literary and linguistic analysis is made closer by the fact that the preliminary units of each kind of study are examined for their recurrent features and the way these features pattern. When the total pattern of the poem emerges, literary analysis proper breaks off. Any further statements are beyond the upper limit of literary structure and are in the area of literary meaning—the area of correlation between the literary structure and known facts of patterned cultural behavior and values. One such statement is worth making. Ransom has called the last two lines a well-schooled theological tag. Pippa breaks her strict analogical pattern to bring *snail* and *God* together. The juxtaposition does not correlate with the way we expect theologians to talk about God. It correlates, instead, with the way we expect children to talk of Him, in concrete and simple terms. Pippa's statement also correlates with our belief that simplicity like hers often contains insights somehow better than those found in the words of the most philosophically sophisticated. One is tempted to find, in the breaking of the pattern Browning has established for her, a sort of model of the cultural contradiction in our attitudes toward children. We treat them as not yet perfected human beings; yet we remember the biblical "out of the mouths of babes and sucklings."[3]

It remains only to state the differences between Ransom's method and that used here. Ransom is structural in his approach but uses semantically defined units without having worked through the formal linguistic differentia. His method is therefore similar to that of traditional grammar, where a formal word class, such as nouns, is defined in terms of the semantic content of the class. In contrast, the analysis given here rests on one of the most basic assumptions in linguistics, that it is form which gives meaning and not meaning which gives form. Ransom's assumptions are commonly used by critics; those used here, by linguists. Since the two sets of assumptions are correlated with differing kinds of activities, it is impractical to measure which set is the more reasonable. Fortunately the two analyses can be measured otherwise. They must be assumed to be significantly different since one cannot be mechanically translated into the other. If different, both cannot be true; one must be more complete, more consistent, and more simple than the other. Evaluation may be left to the reader.

Chapter Four
An Analysis of *The Windhover*:
An Experiment in Method

The Windhover:
  To Christ our Lord

I caught this morning morning's minion, king-
    dom of daylight's dauphin, dapple-dawn-drawn Falcon, in
        his riding
Of the rolling level underneath him steady air, and striding
High there, how he rung upon the rein of a wimpling wing
In his ecstasy! then off, off forth on swing,
    As a skate's heel sweeps smooth on a bow-bend: the hurl
        and gliding
Rebuffed the big wind. My heart in hiding
Stirred for a bird,—the achieve of, the mastery of the thing!

Brute beauty and valour and act, oh, air, pride, plume, here
    Buckle! AND the fire that breaks from thee then, a billion
Times told lovelier, more dangerous, O my chevalier!

    No wonder of it: shéer plód makes plough down sillion
Shine, and blue-bleak embers, ah my dear,
    Fall, gall themselves, and gash gold-vermilion.

GERARD MANLEY HOPKINS

The task I have set myself is not the discovery of new meanings in Hopkins's poem—it has been so widely studied that we rather suffer from a plethora than a paucity of interpretations. I shall try instead to work out some principles that will enable me to choose between alternatives in a fashion that will be systematic. My interest is double: first, in such principles of method as may emerge and, second, in their contribution to the elucidation of the poem by presenting a unified and logical whole.

The analysis is based on a number of assumptions. First, it is assumed that a poem, like a painting or a molecule, has structure. That is, the parts occur in

Note: This essay was originally published in *PMLA* 70 (1955): 968–978.

such a fashion that their relations can be described and used for prediction of recurrence. It follows that the analyst does his best to discover this structure and to make a statement of it. The statement is not something imposed on the poem by the analyst but a theory similar to any analytical hypothesis and subject to testing and rejection by the general criteria of logical analysis: completeness, consistency, and simplicity.

Second, poems are a subclass of utterances included within the larger class of all instances of language use. It follows from this that it ought, at least ideally, to be worthwhile to turn to the science of linguistics to see if this activity, which has as its goal the systematic analysis of language and language use, has anything to contribute in method or results to the analysis of poetry. In linguistics it has been found fruitful to work from observable, external, and formal characteristics to the admittedly more important, but certainly vaguer, resultant qualities of meaning. In literary analysis, likewise, might it not be well to work from formal and observable characteristics toward meanings? This formalist approach is that adopted in the analysis which follows. I shall work from the identification of smaller entities, the evidence for which is to be found in the minutiae of language symbols, to the larger relations, the evidence for which is more broadly structural and less concerned with technical linguistic details. Such a procedure is parallel to the analysis of a sentence, first, into its smaller entities and, then, into larger constituents in discoverable relationships.[1]

The utility of a formal approach can be demonstrated in the first line, where the unwary reader is presented with a minor difficulty in the unpunctuated series "morning morning's minion." The quickest way to demonstrate the meaning is to give it the proper stress and juncture pattern by reading it aloud. "I cáught thĭs mórning/môrnĭng's mínĭon." Once heard, the sequence is established as a familiar and meaningful one. Discussion of the syntax will not make it meaningful unless the discussion also results in the audible pattern which we have been trained to interpret. The pattern of juncture and stress not only establishes the meaning, it immediately demonstrates a point about Hopkins's metrical practice as well. Like all good English poets, Hopkins is varying his poetic stresses. English has four grades of structural stress, which are reduced to two in poetry. The middle grades of stress, secondary and tertiary, are treated as poetic strongs if surrounded by weaker stresses; poetic weaks if surrounded by stronger. In addition, the sequence illustrates a principle governing repetition in English poetry. When repetition of phrases or contiguous words occurs, it must be accompanied by a change in the stress-and-juncture pattern if it is to be successful. It is noteworthy, for instance, that this is the basic device of the triolet.

The next difficulty is one that is a sort of printer's horror. One will note that Hopkins divided his line so as to break the word *kingdom* in two. The alliterating unit in the second line is /d/; so it is probable that the division was intentional. Some modern editors miss it, however, printing *kingdom* unbroken. What are we to say of a poet who alliterates the bound and usually weakly stressed morpheme *-dom* with stressed forms like *daylight*? Admittedly the practice breaks with established convention, and whether you like it or not probably depends on whether you like your art radical or conservative. But how is the sequence to be read? I suggest that it should be read thus: "kíng/ dòm ŏf dâylìght's dáuphĭn." The word *kingdom* in normal speech has a plus juncture, which is required by the sequence velar nasal dental stop.[2] Since the line end falls after *king-*, this plus juncture is strengthened to a single bar, and the normally weak *-dom* gets tertiary stress. This is not a totally unnatural way of talking. We can, for instance, treat a word like *childhood* in this fashion, getting such an utterance as "This is my chíld/hòod" in place of the usual "This is my chíldhŏod." At any rate, whether you regard the device as a legitimate poetic innovation or as a license that results in a blemish, the sequence "-dom of daylight's dauphin" gives three poetic feet, all trochaic, ascending in regular order through the three grades of stress: tertiary, secondary, and primary.

The phrase "dapple-dawn-drawn Falcon" is marked by an intricate design of repetition of sound;[3] the first three words alliterate in /d/; the middle pair also rhyme in /-ɔhn/; and the last assonates with them in /ɔh/. The initial problem is the stress pattern. A parallel for this series is "Fall, gall . . . gash" in the last line. In this second example of joined alliteration and rhyme, the three quoted words not only are all poetic strongs but also receive the same grade of structural stress, as seems appropriate for the part of the pattern where the adornment is most carefully linked. The same reasoning applies to the phrase we are discussing. Additional evidence comes from Hopkins's spelling, where the first three words are treated alike, all being separated by hyphens. Alliteration and spelling both suggest level stress, namely, "dâpplĕ- dâwn-drâwn Fálcŏn."

The phrase would have been clearer had he adopted either one of two alternative stress patterns: "dâpplĕdàwn-drâwn Fálcŏn," or "dâpplĕ-dâwndrawn Fálcŏn." The first would indicate that "dapple" modifies "dawn," the second that it modifies "Falcon." Apparently Hopkins avoided both of these patterns in order to heighten the alliterative effect. The partial ambiguity resulting has created a crux for critics, who have chosen to interpret "dapple" as modifying either "dawn" or "Falcon" according to individual preferences for one or the other resultant meaning. I believe, however, that the ambiguity can be resolved by an examination of the formal characteristics of the phrase.

"Drawn" is shown to be a participle by the occurrence of the ending /-n/. This being so, it forces the interpretation that the preceding word is a noun, in normal syntactic relation to the following participle. Such noun-participle phrases make up unitary modifying elements, rather than a series of modifiers in which each element independently modifies the head of the phrase. They also are an exception to the general rule that elements which make unit modifiers require stress reduction. The participial element being marked by the ending, phrases of this type can occur with variant stress patterns without ambiguity. A similar phrase is "bird haunted glen." This is more usual in the pattern "bîrd hàuntĕd glén," but may also occur as "bîrd hâuntĕd glén." Critics have usually agreed with the syntactic analysis thus far presented and have taken "dawn-drawn" as a unit. With "dapple," however, the situation is different. The only way in which it could be shown to modify "dawn" would be to treat the two as a unit modifier with tertiary stress on the second (or first) word. Such a stress pattern could easily have been shown in spelling by closing up to "dappledawn," which Hopkins did not do. I believe, therefore, that formal evidence points to the conclusion that "dapple" is separate and must modify "Falcon." Similarly, I know of no formal evidence that points in the other direction.

However, "dawn-drawn" establishes merely the syntactic relation between the noun and participle; it does not establish the exact semantic relation. A participial phrase always has a substitute form consisting of participle, preposition, and noun. The ambiguity comes from the fact that we do not know which preposition to choose if we expand to this fuller form. Several are possible: *by*, *toward*, *from*, for instance. On the score of probability we will stand the best chance of being right if we settle for *by*, the commonest. But we are not helped much, since the phrase "drawn by dawn" is still ambiguous. I see no way to tell whether the best substitute for *drawn* is *attracted* or *sketched*. The individual reader can make his own arbitrary choice, but I believe that he must choose and cannot keep both meanings.[4] Instances occur in this poem where multiple meanings must be recognized but only when we find positive evidence for more than one interpretation. Multiple meaning is not acceptable when it is merely a choice between two meanings which are both formally and structurally satisfactory.

In the unusual word order of

> . . . his riding
> Of the rolling level underneath him steady air . . .
> . . . sheer plod makes plough down sillion
> Shine . . .

the peculiarity consists in putting all modifiers, even those that are phrasal units, before the noun or verb as in German. Normal order would be: the rolling, level air, steady underneath him, /sheer plod makes plough shine down sillion. In the first sequence, two phrases have been rearranged; in the second, only one. I cannot hope to see into Hopkins's mind and intentions, but it is possible to point to reasons that might have led him to adopt this un-English order. In our poetry, in marked contrast to the practice of many communities, we value novelty and feel that departure from the normal enhances poetic qualities because it forces the reader to pay close attention. Also, a structural reason emerges from the second sequence. In prose order, "shine down sillion," the verb gets only secondary stress, and the primary stress falls on "sillion." In the order Hopkins has adopted, the primary stress falls on "shine." Hopkins is talking about the surprising emergence of beauty, and the central part of his image is, therefore, the verb. His order, then, brings the stress pattern into closer accord with the logical structure of his phrase. In the first sequence, if we can reason from the second, "air" was for him the important word, and he rearranged accordingly. It might be argued that Hopkins rearranged for no such specific reasons but merely for an appeal to the ear. The phrases do indeed appeal to the ear, but such experiments succeed in their appeal only if something specific is gained by them.

Up to this point I have concerned myself with matters of stress and word order; now I shall discuss, though very briefly, broader structural problems. I have said earlier that purely linguistic matters, such as the stress and word order discussed so far, belong below the threshold of literary structure. I have also said that these linguistic items are then examined in relation to each other and to the whole of the poem to see what patterns emerge. Also, other items belong definitely to the structure of literature, such as statements, images, and figures, which also show patterned relationships to each other and to the whole. Finally, then, we find an area outside the poem itself, in which occur all the correlations between the literary structure and the value system of the community.

The linguistic material, which I have defined as being below the threshold of literary structure, is all too often slighted on the assumptions that it has little relation to literary study and that the contents of the level preliminary to literary study is solely cultural information. That is, knowledge of Renaissance Neoplatonism is thought of as background for the study of Elizabethan sonnets. This kind of material is indeed a proper part of the preliminary level as long as it is treated as factual information. On the other hand, as soon as it is treated as a part of the value system of the culture, it then belongs not below the threshold of literature but beyond its ceiling—an outside end result.

The point just discussed is of crucial importance, since it is very easy to fall into circularity in such matters by confusing result with cause. For instance, I recently asked a student about the phrase in the "Voyage to Brobdingnag" applied by the giant to humankind—a "race of little odious vermin."[5] The question was how the particularly powerful effect of the phrase was created. The answer was that the two adjectives modified "vermin" with equal force. Asked how one could recognize the equal force of the adjectives, the student replied that one recognized it by what the phrase meant. In order to escape the petitio principii, one would have needed to say that the equal modifying force of the adjectives, instead of a situation where the first adjective modified the combination of second adjective and noun, was produced by the shift in order from the normal "odious little vermin" to that used by Swift.

In what follows I shall try to give a detailed model of Hopkins's poem, keeping within what I believe to be the area of literary structure proper. And incidentally, since literature offers an increased possibility of structural analysis over that offered by casual speech, such analyses as these I am attempting should be useful to students of linguistics as well as to those of literature.

The first structural problem is the relation between the six nouns in

> Brute beauty and valour and act, oh, air, pride, plume, here
> Buckle!

The relations can be worked out in terms of describable contexts in which it is probable that each of these nouns would occur. The first set can be numbered

>   1   2   3
> Brute beauty and valour and act.

If we go on to the second set, the most readily identifiable context is that of ethical meaning, in which words like *valour* and *pride* are highly probable. That is to say, number 2 in the second set goes with number 2 in the first. But number 1 in the first half does not go very well with number 1 in the second. On the other hand, in discourse about birds, *beauty* and *plume* are quite predictable. That is, number 1 goes with number 3. What about the remaining pair: *act* and *air*? They fit if we assume the context is flight. These three contexts redefine the set of nouns as "bird," "flight," "meaning," and show them in a surprising but symmetrical 1–2–3:3–2–1 order.

A far more serious difficulty is the meaning of the verb "Buckle!" It has been proposed by W. H. Gardner and others that the verb is imperative. We can here use the technique of discourse analysis, in which meaning is defined as the most probable substitute, controlled by the most frequent sequences, rather than merely the most frequent items. The structure of Hopkins's sentence is a series of nouns followed by a verb. This is the pattern of an indicative sentence in which the nouns are the subjects; it is not the normal construction of an imperative sentence. Thus, "the doors and windows open" will inevitably be taken as an indicative but as an imperative only if something overt in the context forces that interpretation. The occurrence of an exclamation mark, as in Hopkins's sentence, is not such an overt mark, since both indicative and imperative sentences can be so punctuated. Hopkins's syntax is daring enough, it is true, but his successful innovations give us observable clues for interpretation. In the absence of such a clue, there seems no need for departing from the probable in interpretation. We shall therefore reject the suggestion that the verb is imperative—as being possible but unlikely.

I can take next a group of three meanings suggested by Gardner. He takes first the meaning "bend, crumple up under weight or strain," then, by supplying adverbs, formulates three "relevant and complementary meanings of 'Buckle!'—buckle within (discipline), buckle to (labour), buckle under (sacrifice)."[6] Without arguing the legitimacy of supplying adverbs that are not there, or the translation of the phrases once thus constructed, I think it can still be shown that none of these meanings fits very well structurally. The subjects have been shown to be "bird," "flight," and "meaning." I doubt if such a triple subject can be said to be disciplining something, though it possibly is itself disciplined to produce unity. But even if this second sense is the one meant, the suggestion does not fit well with the last figure in the poem, that of the embers. Again, the kestrel may be said to be laboring in carrying out its normal office, and, though this meaning would fit with the figure of the plowman, once again, it would not fit with the embers. As for sacrifice, I do not see that the kestrel is sacrificing anything. The three suggestions seem to be drawn from knowledge of Hopkins's life and religious experience and to lack support within the poem itself.

Far more interesting and attractive is a suggestion from William R. Steinhoff.[7] The flight of the kestrel is characterized by a sudden dive, in which the bird drops on its prey like a falling stone. In current ornithological literature, the flight is said to "buckle." It is possible to argue that knowledge of the bird's flight is a necessary part of the subject and that this interpretation enhances the accuracy of the description. But on the other hand, nowhere in the poem is a reference made to the dive unless it be in the passage under discussion. Unless this passage cannot be explained otherwise, introduction of the dive involves an extra hypothesis. Further, if *dive* is the meaning, it immediately falls into relation with "more dangerous" in the line below. It thus gets some immediate support, but it makes the central image of this section of the poem one of cruelty and attack. Images of suffering occur in the latter part of poem but images of attack do not. Therefore, even at the expense of some regret, it seems necessary to reject the suggestion for reasons of simplicity and because it ultimately lacks structural support. The suggestion again seems to me one which involves interpretation by extraliterary evidence alone and to be weak for that reason.

There remain two more possibilities. *Buckle* can mean "fasten," as in "I buckled my belt," and it can mean "bend to the point of breaking," as in "the walls buckled when the fire reached them." If we look at the preceding context, we find Hopkins is talking about bird, flight, and meaning. These can be expected to create a unity. In terms of the preceding, the meaning "fasten" is strongly suggested. But if we look ahead, we find "the fire that breaks from thee then." Not only does the passage contain the second possible substitute for *buckle*, but it is also saying that unity so far transcends the parts that it may be said to break out of them.

Students of literature have been saying, at least since the days of Alexandria, that literature is richer in meanings than is ordinary language. Nowadays, however, it is possible to go to communication theory for an account of how multiple meanings work and thus to give a theoretical explanation that is perhaps more understandable and offers more possibility of verification. Speech, say the communication theorists, is interpreted in accord with a process called a Markov chain; that is, a chain of continually differentiated probabilities, where the highest probability is always treated as if it were 100 percent. Thus, since *the* is an extremely frequent sentence beginner, a sentence beginning / və/ would be strongly subject to mishearing. In turn, once *the* is heard, then the next item will be expected to be a noun rather than a verb. The human brain is such an efficient calculator of highest differential probabilities in such a chain that we reach a point where we no longer really need to listen. But it is instructive that the probabilities are never really 100 percent, so that a hearer can always make serious mistakes with forms of low frequency. Suppose I say, "I've been reading Ham——." It is most likely that it will be filled out with "-let," but there is always the possibility of "-ilton."[8]

One of the characteristics of literature in our own and all other communities is its permanence. It can be read over and over again or, in preliterate communities, recited from memory. Ordinary speech is ephemeral, meant to be reacted to and forgotten. Markov chains in speech, therefore, work mostly forward and over a fairly short span. In literature they can also work backward, and there can be more than one chain running at a time, so that a given item can have one meaning in one span, a different one in a second. The check on a proposed multiple meaning is then the occurrence of two or more sequences that measurably affect probability of interpretation, as *the* affects the choice between noun and verb in the example above. In deciding on the meaning of *buckle* I have already pointed to two such spans, one working forward and suggesting "fasten," the other working backward and suggesting "break." The likelihood of two meanings is increased by the fact that the two meanings are symmetrical since they are opposites.

In the formula of address "O my chevalier! " there can also be clarification by double meaning. It has been interpreted by I. A. Richards as referring to the poet. Even though the poem is an intensely personal one, the poet does not elsewhere address himself, so that to make the formula refer to Hopkins is to isolate it from any span which might give it support. On the more immediate level, I think there is little doubt that the formula refers to the bird, and the support for it is that the bird has earlier been compared to a rider. The longer span is that made up of the dedication and the address "ah my dear" below. In this sequence, as many critics have suggested, identification with Christ is highly probable. The identification certainly has consequences for the interpretation of larger structural units, but to these I shall return later.

Richards goes on to discuss two more phrases:

> [My heart in hiding.] Why in hiding? Hiding from what? Does this link up with 'a billion times told lovelier, more dangerous, O my chevalier!' What is the greater danger, and what the less? I should say the poet's heart is in hiding from Life, has chosen a safer way, and that the greater danger is the greater exposure to temptation and error than a more sheltered course (sheltered by Faith?) brings with it. Another, equally plausible reading would be this: Renouncing the glamour of the outer life of adventure the poet transfers its qualities of audacity to the inner life. (*Here* is the bosom, the inner consciousness.) The greater danger is that to which the moral hero is exposed. Both readings may be combined, but pages of prose would be required for a paraphrase of the result.[9]

It may be unkind to take a man to task for something he said in 1926, but this interpretation is certainly not simple, as his last sentence seems to admit. It also draws heavily on the extraliterary and seems to me not supported by entities in the poem itself.

As for "my heart in hiding," I should interpret: "the poet's emotional being (heart) has withdrawn seeking safety (hiding)." The notion of safety reappears in "more dangerous," a phrase applied to the sight of the bird, which has stirred his heart. It is the bird, then, which is more dangerous as its beauty increases, more dangerous because the beauty breaks through Hopkins's defenses. All this is carried in the poem itself and is not an explanation for which I have gone to extraliterary data. The explanation fits with known extraliterary facts, it is true, since Hopkins had withdrawn from the world and might well fear a sight that could draw him back. Correspondence with the extraliterary is a confirmation of a prediction, however, and should not be a primary analytic tool.

We are now ready to take up the major structural entities and relations in the poem. The latter section of the poem is built on two figures: the plodding plowman produces the unexpected brightness of the plowshare; embers fall and produce the unexpected brightness of gold-vermilion. Both deal with unexpected beauty, greater than its parts. Both are analogies for the bird in flight: as plowshare is to plowman, so flight is to hawk. Trouble comes, however, if we try to push the analogies further. We have been told that the beauty of the hawk is dangerous; does this analogy apply to plowshare and embers? I do not believe so, since then the additional figures would be merely repetitious, and there would be difficulty in the identification of the bird with Christ. An element of contradiction exists between the antecedents and the result in both figures, which is new. In the plowman figure dullness produces brightness; the embers, when wounded, produce not pain but new life. The implication in both figures is that the whole is not merely greater than its parts but is a good which is unpredictable from the parts. Carried back to the hawk, the analogies imply that the danger may be a greater good on some higher level.

There remain the structural implications of the identification of the bird with Christ. The immediate suggestion is that Christ, who is mentioned at the climax of the description of the hawk and again in the embers figure, alone understands what is to Hopkins a paradox and a mystery. In larger import, the identification can only mean that the bird in flight is a symbol and analogy for Christ. Hopkins does not develop the analogy; he merely implies that one exists. To develop it, however, will carry the analyst into the extraliterary sphere, and I shall therefore merely suggest the general area in which I am reasonably sure the analogy must lie. Christ in this world suffered Crucifixion, emerging therefrom a billion times told lovelier. The Christ as God is dangerous to sinful, slothful man, but on the higher level—the only one that matters—he is the Savior.

The microliterary content of the poem may now be stated in sequence:

1. The poem is dedicated to Christ.[10]
2. The hawk in flight is like a rider and horse and like a skater and skate.
3. Bird, flight, and meaning become a totality, which in turn becomes a much greater beauty and a danger.
4. The bird is directly addressed and identified with Christ.
5. The humble plowman produces the unexpected beauty of the plowshare.

6. Dull embers wound themselves into new brightness.
7. Christ is again addressed and again identified with the bird.

Since this content represents a pattern, it would be possible to demonstrate its symmetry by a spatial diagram, though only at the expense of unfamiliar symbolism. I shall therefore try to explain without diagraming. The introductory section of the poem is section 2, which consists of two equations with balanced two-part halves: hawk and air equal rider and horse. Section 3 is not an equation but a three-part progression: flight becomes totality, which becomes beauty and danger. The last part of the poem is sections 5 and 6, which are strictly parallel to each other. They can be called sums: plowman plus motion becomes brightness; embers plus wounding become brightness. In a kind of back reference, sections 5 and 6 are equated with section 3, revising our understanding of it.

Sections 1, 4, and 7 are, so to speak, parallel with the structure here outlined and are repeated statements that this microliterary form is duplicated in a corresponding extraliterary structure. The structural statement makes clear where the complexity and difficulty of the poem lie. They do not lie in the overall structure, which is severely simple, but in the ornate and intricate details.[11]

Part Two
Types of Meaning and Imagery

Chapter Five
Poetry and Stylistics

All the world knows that poetry is to be enjoyed and that enjoyment is its sole reason for being. When no one enjoys a poem, it is promptly forgotten. I have no wish to disagree with such a set of self-evident truisms. I wish instead to point out that, true as such statements may be, they are not the whole truth about poetry and that to assume that they are the whole truth not only makes us misunderstand the nature and function of poetry but also blinds us to much of the beauty of poetry and dulls us to its enjoyment.

For one thing, if all that matters about poetry is the enjoyment and if enjoyment is its only measure, we are immediately faced with a question— whose enjoyment? We live now in a splintered kind of society in which each one of us must choose between a myriad of competing groups—we can be Republicans or Democrats; Episcopalians, Baptists, Catholics, or Mormons; scientists, businessmen, soldiers, or technicians. It is less and less possible for any one man to embrace the experience of more than a few of these competing groups. The result is that the broad base of shared experience—the property of the whole community—which was the foundation of truly national poetry like the Homeric epics, is no longer characteristic of our society. Poetry speaks, not to the whole community, but to this or that splinter of it at a time. We have western poets, eastern poets, English poets, American poets, religious poets, antireligious poets, intellectual poets, and antiintellectual poets. We even have groups who are antipoetic and believe that all poets and all who enjoy poetry belong to a splinter group. We have no poets and no poetry that can speak clearly and without necessary interpretation to all speakers of English as Homer spoke to all the Hellenes.

Note: This essay was presented as a public lecture at the University of Virginia, in one of the Peters Rushton Seminars in Contemporary Prose and Poetry, September 21, 1956. It was privately printed in *Essays in Literary Analysis* (Austin: Dailey Diversified Services, 1965) and was reprinted in *Essays on the Language of Literature*, ed. Seymour Chatman and Samuel Levin (New York: Houghton Mifflin Co., 1967), pp. 385–397. The version given here has been considerably revised in the first portion, and one of the three poems originally discussed, "The Soul selects her own Society," by Emily Dickinson, has been omitted. It is fully discussed in "Figurative Structure and Meaning: Two Poems by Emily Dickinson," chap. 12. The later version of that analysis supersedes that of this essay.

If poetry is thus no longer an art with the wide and unquestioned appeal it had in the days of scops and troubadours, the critic and the teacher of litera- ture find themselves in an uncomfortable position. Neither can any longer say without fear of contradiction that every speaker of English enjoys this poem deeply and that, therefore, it is great. Nor can they measure a poem by the permanence of its appeal since many readers reject older literature as hard to understand. The differentiation that has splintered our contemporary literature has cut literature off from the past as well. We cannot, certainly, assume that young people are automatically equipped to read the poetry of Wyatt and Sur- rey. To read the poetry of Wyatt and Surrey it is as necessary to study it as it is to study any poetry from a community different from our own—it is always necessary to know the code before we can get the message. Those who have faced the task of teaching poetry in contemporary America sooner or later begin to ask themselves embarrassing questions about who enjoys the various kinds of poetry they teach. T. S. Eliot appeals to sophisticates; Joyce Kilmer, to Babbitts. Perhaps there is an easy answer for those who know which group is more valuable to our society and which group should, therefore, be the ar- biter of taste. Yet many teachers will admit that we cannot judge between groups in any high-handed and authoritarian fashion and that we cannot even take the judgments handed down to us from a time when our society was less complex and the poetically excellent was simply defined as what an English gentleman would like.

It would seem that, if we who study poetry are to be able to talk about it to others than the members of our various tiny groups, we should find some other approach than pure enjoyment. We should find, or create, an approach that takes as its aim a secure and demonstrable increase of understanding. Some say that such an approach is impossible without sacrifice of the en- joyment that all agree is the basis of poetry, as it is of all art. To say so is to give a counsel of despair. A more hopeful belief is that understanding is a good in itself and that understanding need not be in conflict with other things that are good. It is not an unreasonable position to say that all things in the world of man and nature can be studied by the human intelligence. True, we shall never reach complete understanding of anything in the world of man and nature. If we should say that it is therefore useless to strive for comprehen- sion, we would abdicate our heritage. Or if we should say that poetry belongs in a world that transcends intelligence and, so, is something that we cannot know, we are confusing the world of man—since poets are men—with the world beyond the world of men, which, indeed, we cannot know.

In this essay I shall once more try to give an approach that is based on un- derstanding and that studies the poem itself, not what kind of readers should enjoy it or how much. I hope, moreover, that such an approach not only may not reduce enjoyment but even increase it and enrich it. Also, as I have often said, what I shall say is in the nature of a hypothesis, delivered with the reservation that, when more is known, what I say now may seem naïve or positively wrong.

I shall begin with a mapping of the field of literary study in relation to a similar map for the field of linguistic study. I have in two of the essays (the analyses of *Pippa's Song* and *The Windhover*) referred briefly to these maps, but it is my intention now to give them in full detail. In mapping the area of linguistics, structural linguists often use the figure of three levels;[1] the lowest and the highest are outside language proper, but each has connections with it. The middle area is that of language per se, within which falls all that we know of its structure. The lowest level is that of the material from which talk is made, that is, sounds and articulations. On this level, sounds are without language function and are mere noises. To use an example described by Edward Sapir a generation ago, we may make nearly the same noise in blowing out a candle as in giving the initial sound of the word *when*.[2] A student of the lowest level of communication, like a sound spectrograph, could describe exactly the physical properties of the sound, but, like the sound spectrograph, he would not know whether the sound was used in the word or in blowing out the candle.

At the highest level, on the other hand, is the nonlinguistic world of objects, actions, states, and relationships. When we establish a correspondence between items of language and something in the real world, we have established meaning—the kind of meaning we can call correspondence meaning. This kind of meaning is what we are most conscious of and which is most important to us.

The area of language proper, which is a sort of island between sounds and articulations on the one hand and meanings on the other, has four sublevels. The first three are fairly obvious. They are, first, the level of patterned and functioning sounds, or phonology; second, the level of patterned and functioning word-elements, or morphology, the product of which is the word as it appears in isolation; and, third, the level of syntax, the patterning and functioning of words in relation to each other, the product of which is the sentence, again as it appears in isolation. In describing the fourth and last of the sublevels, however, I am departing at least slightly from earlier formulations. The fourth level is that of sentences in relation to each other, the product of which is the structure of discourse. It is characteristic of this level that the structures which comprise it spread, much of the time, over more than one sentence, though it is also true that they may, on occasion, appear within a single sentence.

I have said that the most important kind of meaning is that which I have called correspondence meaning. Another kind of meaning, however, appears on all the levels of the area of language proper and underlies the area of correspondence meaning. This is the kind of meaning that can be described as the quality of partial predictability. That is, if I should use a nonsense word, it would be meaningless because it is outside the system of my language. Being outside the system, it would be impossible for a hearer to predict that I was going to use it. On the other hand, if I should always clear my throat at the end of every sentence, my hearers would soon know exactly when I was going to clear my throat, since they would know, without listening for the throat clearing, that a sentence was ending. In such circumstances, the throat clearing would be totally predictable and, once again, meaningless. Whatever occurs with total and predictable regularity can be disregarded since it can carry no new information.

As for the partial predictability of language items, I can illustrate hurriedly by pointing out that no English word or sentence begins with the sound which is final in *sing*. If we happen to turn on a radio in the middle of a sentence and happen to hear the final sound of *sing* without anything preceding it, we automatically guess that something is ending, not that something is beginning. On the level of words, if we hear the definite article *the*, we again guess, this time that the next word may be a noun or adjective but is not going to be a verb or pronoun. And, finally, on the level of sentence relationships, if we hear "The book is in English," we guess that this particular book has been mentioned in a previous sentence. As for partial predictability in relation to correspondence meaning, note that, if we hear "There's a rabbit in the garden," we expect to be able to check the statement by finding the creature, though we recognize that the statement might be mistaken. If, on the other hand, we hear "There's a hippogriff in the garden," our attempts at checking will be in vain. The act of prediction, being based on an only partial quality, has failed us.

I can now bring this to bear on poetry at last. First, poetic structure is like language structure in being something that can be mapped in terms of levels. Many critics have said that literature may be like language but is somehow more than language and different from it. I believe that such statements are explainable in terms of the diagram that I am describing. As for the likeness, literature can also be described as having three levels. The lower level is not literature but is the material out of which literature is made, as language is made of sounds. Literature has a middle area, which is the area of literary structure and all that we know about it, and it has an upper area, in which the items and, even more, the structures of literature correspond with something on the outside, thus setting up once more the phenomenon of correspondence meaning.

The way in which this map of literary structure differs from the map of language is that the two are not perfectly parallel. What goes into the nonliterary lower level is most of the area of language structure. That is, the material of which literature is made is the sum total of phonology, morphology, and syntax. And it is extremely important to state emphatically that these things are not literature in themselves. The area of the level immediately below language, on the other hand, is totally irrelevant to literature. As the critic W. K. Wimsatt once remarked, the number of vibrations per second in the vowel /æ/ has nothing to do with the way in which *gentleman* is made meaningful in John Ball's couplet

> When Adam delved and Eve span
> Who was then a gentleman?[3]

One of the reasons linguists have suffered justified attacks in the past is that we have often assumed that vowel and consonant counting is the way to show that linguistics is relevant to literature.

I have said that the area of language and its structure is the lowest level for the literary student. In general, the statement is obvious. We all know that it is well to understand the grammar and vocabulary of a poem before we begin to dogmatize about it. We have all had students, for instance, who did not know that in Shakespeare's song about *Fancie*, the word means the first stage of love rather than an image in the mind, or the like.[4] Similarly we have all corrected students who suppose that Portia is personifying the candle by her use of *his* in the line "How farre that little candell throwes his beames,"[5] since the pronoun is no more than the Elizabethan equivalent of *its*. Unfortunately, however, critics are often less knowledgeable about the way in which pitch and stress have a bearing on meaning. Still sticking to Shakespeare, I remember correcting a student who was reading aloud from *Othello*, and who read the messenger's line in the first act, "The *Ottamites,* Reueren'd, and Gracious,"[6] without the proper comma intonation, making it mean "The Ottamites [who are] Reueren'd and Gracious," instead of the vocative form addressed to the Duke.

The central area of literary structure falls on the uppermost area of language—the area of sentences and their relations to each other—within the totality of the poem or discourse. A convenient name for this area is style, meaning by that the area of sentence-syntax. I am aware of the many other definitions of style, and I do not wish to quarrel with them. Style and the study of it, stylistics, are convenient designations for an important area, and I shall continue to use them, as I have said. The content of this stylistic area is clearly the area in which many, if not all, literary devices fall. For instance, rhyme and meter extend over the whole of a poem, no matter how many sentences it may contain. Also, it is a truism that much of style consists in congruent selection of vocabulary, as when Henry James is supposed to have said, "If the handle is depressed, egress will be facilitated." The sentence is isolated, it is true, but it is nearly certain that any other sentences in the same discourse would have had vocabulary congruent with what is here. Note how very different the quoted sentence is from another that contains the same information but a very different vocabulary: "Shove the handle down to get out."

I shall not divide the area of literary structure with extreme minuteness, since this is a familiar field. However, it certainly contains at least three major sublevels, one being a phonological area more important to poetry than to prose but by no means lacking in prose. Here belong the structures of rhyme, meter, alliteration, assonance, and the like. The second sublevel is that of congruence in vocabulary, as in the supposed Jamesian sentence quoted above. The third area is a statable total pattern most clearly seen in poetry but also found in prose. By this I mean the kind of patterning that may be analogical or even allegorical or merely a pattern that has recognizable symmetry, as when Edgar Allan Poe in the poem *To Helen* says Helen calls the wanderer, first, to ancient Greece, then to ancient Rome, and that these taken together make "Holy Land."[7]

When we pass to the uppermost level, literature characteristically shows more sublevels than does ordinary language. There we find the simple correspondence level of information, real or fictitious. Thus the statement that Kubla Khan built a palace has simple correspondence meaning. There is also a second level, that of correspondence between the total structure of the poem and the outside nonliterary world. *Kubla Khan* has a correspondence of the total structure with the dream world that Coleridge conjured up. The song *Tell me where is fancie bred* has a total structural meaning corresponding to the philosophical structure of Elizabethan love lore. And, of course, allegorical works like *Pilgrim's Progress* or *In the Penal Colony* show this total structural correspondence meaning minutely elaborated. The final level of meaning is that which is most peculiarly proper to literature and the presentation of which is the most important purpose of literary art. This is the level of correspondence with cultural values.

It should not be thought that these levels are necessarily absent in ordinary uses of language, though it is clear that, in a simple sentence like "It's going to rain today," only simple correspondence meaning is present. Also, the level of style is essentially absent in such a sentence, which characteristically is apt to be isolated and not a part of a unified discourse. In a set of directions for using a mechanical tool, however, clear stylistic structures are apt to be

Table 1.   Levels of language and literature

Level	Language	Literature	Level
Uppermost nonlanguage	Correspondence meaning	Cultural values Structural and analogical meaning Correspondence meaning	Uppermost most nonliterary
Language proper	Structure and function of sentences, discourse structure or style	Content structures of literature Phonological structures of literature (rhyme, meter, etc.)	Literature proper
	Structure and function of words, syntax Structure and function of meaningful elements, morphology Structure and function of sounds, phonology	Language as material of literature	Lowest nonliterary
Lowest nonlanguage	Articulations and sounds	Irrelevant	

found, and, certainly, in a culture like our own, which is strongly mechanical in orientation, a good portion of cultural values are found as well. Yet, characteristically, the several levels of meaning are central to literature and therefore strongly elaborated. In ordinary language they may be absent or rudimentary. The levels of language and literature can now be mapped as shown in table 1.

This long description of the relation of literature and language can be concluded by pointing out that the kind of meaning that consists of partial predictability of occurrence also occurs in the various levels of literature just as it does in language. Thus the phonological structures of poetry show recurrence and are thus partially predictable. The occurrence of "June" in the tenth syllable, to give a hackneyed example, predicts that the twentieth syllable will be "moon," or the like—at any rate that the sound sequence /-uwn/ will recur. But I should wish to be emphatic in stating that the phonological structures do not have imitative value except very briefly and relatively unimportantly and are thus devoid of any kind of correspondence meaning.[8]

For the content structures of literature, note that congruity of vocabulary occurs over the whole of the discourse and strongly influences the occurrence of individual words. Similarly, the occurrence of a type of construction, such as the balanced sentences of Edward Gibbon, influences the type of sentence structure just as congruity of vocabulary influences the occurrence of words.

Poetry, more than any other kind of literature, heightens and exploits stylistic structures and devices. Rhyme and meter are phonological devices and structures spreading over the whole of the poem. Poetic diction is a special stylistic type of lexicon, and the figures and images of poetry are stylistic devices of content, in which we rightly feel that the real heart of the poem often lies. This stylistic heightening makes possible an aim that the poet almost always holds—he tries to transcend the linguistic meanings by giving stylistic structures which change them and add to them so that the whole of the poem has meaning, which would escape us if we considered only its parts.

One of the ways in which modern poetry—that kind where *modern* might almost be in quotation marks—differs from traditional poetry is that the poet often says something that would be quite ungrammatical on the linguistic level, hoping that it will become meaningful on the stylistic level. Thus, E. E. Cummings wrote "anyone lived in a pretty how town."[9] As ordinary English, the line does not make sense. Yet, as we read the poem as a whole, the general stylistic structure enables us to translate it approximately as "an ordinary man lived in an ordinary, pretty kind of town." Cummings has played a sort of game of linguistics against stylistics; yet the game is not so different from the ordinary procedure of the poet; its strangeness consists only in that he adopts the linguistically unpredictable deliberately.

In bringing this fairly extensive discussion of theory to bear on two individual poems, I shall confine myself to the use that the poems make of a single stylistic device. The device is analogy. Nothing is new in saying that poets make use of analogies; the familiar terms *metaphor* and *simile* describe two main types of them. What I shall try to show is that development of analogy is the device by which the poet gives stylistic unity to his poem and makes it meaningful in ways beyond the meaning of sober everyday sentences. We shall see that the device is characteristic of poetry and that it may lead to stylistic meanings almost as much in conflict with linguistic ones as were the stylistic and linguistic meanings in the line from Cummings.

Our first poem is this from Carl Sandburg:

LOST

Desolate and lone
All night long on the lake
Where fog trails and mist creeps,
The whistle of a boat
Calls and cries unendingly,
Like some lost child
In tears and trouble
Hunting the harbour's breast
And the harbour's eyes.[10]

The poem obviously offers no very great difficulty in understanding. The
whistle of a boat reminds the poet of a lost child crying, and that seems clear
enough. The analogy is overt, since the poet tells us flatly "like some lost
child." Yet the simple overall structure is not quite all that is here since the
separate parts of the two halves of the analogy are brought into a more detailed relationship with each other. The whistle is to the boat on the lake as
sobs are to the child away from its mother. The phrase "the harbour's
breast" gives us a compressed subanalogy—breast is to mother as X is to harbor. Note that we are left to supply the identity of the missing X—one of the
two places in the poem where we meet such an implicit analogy. The X is not
hard to supply; in this case it is the mooring at which the boat comes to rest.
The second X, of course, is in the compressed phrase "harbour's eyes,"
where eyes are to mother as X is to the harbor—evidently the harbor's
lights.[11]
Sandburg's little poem is obviously a simple one. If it has interest, it must
somehow be in the analogies around which it is built. We can point to a
number of ways in which these analogies are interesting. The first one is of no
great literary importance, though of interest to us in this kind of study. By
throwing together items that belong to the two halves of his analogy—*eyes*,
which belongs with the child-mother half, and *harbour,* which belongs with
the boat-harbor half—Sandburg gives us a phrase that is compressed—"harbour's eyes"—and leaves one term in his proportional analogy
as an unsolved X, which the reader must supply. The reader can be relied on
to solve it since the structure of the analogy forces the solution. This sort of
unsolved X is one of the principal ways in which an analogy is made to say
something that is there stylistically but linguistically not present at all.
Second, the poem starts with a simple comparison. Probably none of us has
failed to respond to the loneliness of a train or boat whistle at night. The as-
cription of human emotional value to such a sound is a commonplace and

might be considered one of the tritest comparisons a poet could make. It is the points of correspondence, as the single general analogy is worked out in a series of linked subanalogies, that give the poem structure, unity, and some sense of originality. Further, as by now we might expect of a poetic structure, it suggests correspondence with the nonliterary world of cultural values—we can extrapolate from literary structure to a structure of meanings. For me, at least, the lost boat, compared to a child who has lost the security of his mother's breast, suggests an identification with the society we live in. We, too, are lost and long to return to a simpler society in the childhood of the world. The Sandburg poem is simple, indeed, but the stylistic structure is certainly more meaningful than would be the linguistic statement—that boat sounds like a lost child.

The second poem is different from the first because it has been so institutionalized that we accept it, without thinking about it or really reading it, as merely a part of our traditions. Also, it can be read and valued highly without working out the analogies it contains; it can give, indeed, the impression of being completely understood with no analysis at all. The analogies must therefore, if study of them is to be justified, modify or increase the understanding of the poem enough to make their exposition worth the effort and must not spoil our appreciation of the poem.

Composed upon Westminster Bridge, September 3, 1802

Earth has not anything to show more fair:
Dull would he be of soul who could pass by
A sight so touching in its majesty:
This City now doth, like a garment, wear
The beauty of the morning; silent, bare,
Ships, towers, domes, theatres, and temples lie
Open unto the fields, and to the sky;
All bright and glittering in the smokeless air.
Never did sun more beautifully steep
In his first splendour, valley, rock, or hill;
Ne'er saw I, never felt, a calm so deep!
The river glideth at his own sweet will:
Dear God! the very houses seem asleep;
And all that mighty heart is lying still![12]

I do not need to comment on the surface meaning of the poem. All of us recognize that Wordsworth saw the city in unwonted beauty and was moved by it with a religious emotion. All of us can share the emotion. Let us see how study changes our emotion and whether study enriches it.

We can pass over the first three lines as not relevant to our purposes; they contain no important analogies. The first analogy is in the third and fourth lines

> This City now doth, like a garment, wear
> The beauty of the morning;

That is, beauty of the morning is to the city as garment is to X. Only human beings—normally, at least—wear garments. The city is, then, like a human being. The garments are next described:

> . . . silent, bare,
> Ships, towers, domes, theatres, and temples lie
> Open unto the fields, and to the sky;

The garment is not like a suit of clothes or an overcoat. It is such as to reveal the city and its structures. We can express all this by an analogy that builds on the first one: The city wears a garment that reveals its structures as a human being of X type wears a garment that reveals its body. The garment that thus reveals beauty is not the sort of garment we talk about as worn by men or children. It is like the garment of a beautiful woman, and the city is not merely like a human being but like a woman.

The city-woman, further, lies in a calm and beautiful morning sleep. As well as the city and its parts, another set of entities can be found in the poem. The entities are fields, sky, and river. They can easily be grouped as belonging to the non-man-made nature, opposed in principle to the man-made city. A very common attitude in our literature is the idea that God made the country, but man made the town—true or not, we all know the attitude. Yet the relation given here of these representatives of nature is not one of conflict with the city. The city-woman and its structures "lie/Open unto the fields, and to the sky;" and below, "The river glideth at his own sweet will." The analogy can be constructed thus: Nature is to city as X is to woman. I submit, therefore, that language and situation in this poem lead to the conclusion that the final missing X is lover and that nature and city are compared to man and woman in the sleep of lovers.

I am aware enough that these analogies, thus made overt, might be thought of as shocking. Yet, they need not be and should not be. A further statement in the poem throws light on how we are to view the comparison ". . . sun . . ./ In his first splendour." One way of reading this phrase would be to take it as a reference merely to the first light of this particular September 3. But throughout the poem we find hints that the scene is touched by a lost beauty—the air is smokeless, for instance, though presumably Wordsworth's negative statement implies that it was not often so. Wordsworth uses *temples* instead of the more prosaic and realistic *churches* as if he were suggesting a past more beautiful than the usual present.[13] For these reasons, I believe that "first splendour" refers to the dawn of the world rather than to the dawn of September 3. City and nature are as lovers but lovers with an innocence and beauty lost since Eden.[14]

I do not think I need to carry the central city-woman analogy much further into the realm of correspondences and cultural values. It is enough to say that man and nature are reconciled, released, and united as a man and woman are in love. Wordsworth did not often talk so of the works of man, and I think we can agree that he is a greater poet for the vision of a reconciliation, which he grasped that morning on the bridge. The analogies are, I believe, the central structure of the poem—they are the way in which the larger unity of style is made to transcend the limitations of the linguistic statements. Wordsworth's success could not be achieved without them, I feel sure. His success, in turn, is a revealing example of the way in which poetry is language, yet more than language and different from it.

Chapter Six
Analogies, Icons, and Images

There have been many attempts to classify, define, and describe the categories of figures of speech, but, curiously enough, little attention has been paid to the closely related phenomena of imagery. It is the contention of this essay that imagery and figures of speech can be most profitably discussed together and, further, that classification of the types of imagery both can and should be simpler than it often is.

For current description of imagery, it would seem to me that the most successful treatments divide up imagery into the kinds of objects represented, as when Caroline Spurgeon maintains that the essential imagery found in the speeches of the character Macbeth is concerned with ill-fitting clothes[1] or when critics, as they commonly do, point to the imagery of winter storms and destruction making way for spring and renewal in a poem like Shelley's *West Wind*. Less successful, it seems to me, is the common division of imagery into metaphor and simile since, though the difference is easily recognized and defined, it does not seem to me that the distinction reflects anything that is necessarily different in the two types. For instance, it is possible to say equally well that "my love is like a red, red rose" or merely "my red rose love" or "my love, a red, red rose." Aside from the trivial difference that it is (in my idiolect) at least slightly awkward to repeat the adjective twice in a prenominal modifying phrase, there seems no real difference in anything that could affect either the aesthetic qualities or the meaning.

A typical, and very scholarly, grammatical classification of types of imagery is by Christine Brooke-Rose. Miss Brooke-Rose quotes the elaborate classification of Friedrich Brinkmann, dating back to 1878. Brinkmann divides metaphors into nine different types, such as "metaphor with copula *est* and forms of *esse* (she is a rose)," "metaphor by genitive apposition (the fire of love)," and "metaphor contained in the verb." Miss Brooke-Rose says that Brinkmann's classification "is much more confused than [her] abstracted ver-

Note: This essay was given as a lecture at the Bowdoin Symposium on Linguistics and Literature in May of 1967 and was published in *Style* 2 (1968): 203–227. It has been slightly revised for publication in this volume, most importantly in the statements on tropes.

sion'' and that he "makes no use whatever of [his] divisions" in actual discussion.[2] Her own partial classification of metaphors of nominal type results
in five types, all of which are basically grammatical.[3]

1. *Simple Replacement*: An example is "Hopkins: Or is it she cried for *the
crown* then (W[reck of the] D[eutschland] 25, *crown* [of martyrdom])."[4]

2. *The Pointing Formulae*: "The proper term A is mentioned, then replaced by the metaphor B with some demonstrative pointing back to the
proper term (A . . . that B)." Miss Brooke-Rose maintains that a simple demonstrative is one means of calling attention to the replacement. An example is:

> A woman drew her long hair out tight
> And fiddled whisper music on *those strings*.
> W[aste] L[and]. 377–[378].[5]

3. "*The Copula*: A direct statement that A is B, [including] forms such as
to seem, *to call* or *be called*, *to signify*, *to be worth*, *to become*." An example
is:

> This flea is *you* and I, and this
> Our mariage *bed*, and mariage *temple* is . . .
> Donne [*The Flea*, lines 12–13].[6]

4. "*The link with 'To Make'*: a direct statement involving a third party: C
makes A into B." An example is:

> Apollo's upward fire
> Made every eastern cloud a silvery *pyre*
> [John Keats,] End[ymion 1, lines 94–95].[7]

5. "*The Genitive* (in the very wide sense of provenance from)." An example is:

> Although the summer sunlight gild
> Cloudy *leafage* of the sky, . . .
> Yeats [*Vacillation* 5, lines 1–2].[8]

When it is realized that Miss Brooke-Rose also takes up metaphors from the
point of view of part of speech employed, it is clear that her classification is of
considerable complexity. I have quoted her classification at some length,
because I believe it is possible to collapse it into three types, without respect
to whether we are dealing with nominal, verbal, or adjectival types. I believe,
further, that at the same time it will be possible to define both figure and
image more exactly than has usually been done and to throw some light on
how they work.

A first statement is that the several forms of imagery and figure belong to the area of discourse analysis, the area that I have elsewhere defined as that of style.[9] The delimitations of the area of linguistics to that which falls within the borders of the sentence, of stylistics to relations between items, or, indeed, of items themselves that are not thus limited to single sentences are useful to the investigations pursued in this volume and are therefore used without apology. One point for clarification is that occurrence of alternatives within the borders of the sentence is often a matter of choice, so that style is sometimes defined as a choice of alternatives. For instance, whether we say "six eggs" or "a half dozen eggs" is quite irrelevant as long as we consider the single sentence in which the two items occur, though if we consider the context of each, the choice of one item over the other may be strongly affected. That is, if the context is one in which we are enumerating single items (five apples, seven oranges, etc.), it is likely that we should say "six eggs." If we are enumerating things in units of dozens (two dozen cakes, one dozen oranges, etc.), the choice is more likely to be "a half dozen eggs."

Stylistic occurrences may be found within the border of a single sentence, of course, but remain stylistic if the pattern they show is such that it can recur in a wider context. A stylistic occurrence, furthermore, may be either forced or chosen by the user. An example of a stylistic recurrence that is forced is the fact that a proper name must be replaced in its later occurrences by a pronoun, whether or not the later occurrences are in the same sentence as the first. Such forced stylistic occurrences are of very little aesthetic interest, since they always occur in one way only and lack alternate occurrences with which they may be compared. A pattern which is not forced may be said to be the result of choice, though the choice is likely to be governed by the user's skill in producing consistency. Obviously, also, the stylistic recurrences that are the result of the user's choice are of primary interest to the critic, since they alone offer alternatives giving opportunity for value judgments. I should like to repeat, however, since I have not always been understood on the subject, that, first, the mere fact that a given occurrence is forced by rule is no proof that it is not a stylistic matter. On the other hand, a writer or speaker who constructs a pattern in which all parts seem so right as to be inevitable is also making use of choice, even though that choice has been powerfully affected by the other items which occur in the pattern.

A minor difficulty, however, exists with the first of the types of figures and images that I shall take up. This is the simple transfer (or possible transfer) of a single term. If, for instance, I speak of a *marble brow* or *raven hair*, there does not seem to be anything more extended in these constructions than the occurrence of isolated prenominal modifiers, without any relation to what occurs or does not occur in the surrounding discourse. Yet it is quite likely that such terms will occur in clusters, as when I speak of *raven hair*, *pearly teeth*, and *rosy lips*. It is obvious that such clusters can easily be extended to wider contexts, so that they can be spoken of as stylistic. Further, as I shall try to show, it is in just such clusters that we find stylistic support for a transferred term and that the term is most likely to have some real significance and, therefore, be a genuine image. The occurrence of transferred items as individual vocabulary occurrences is therefore a good deal like other vocabulary items. Whether we speak of an object, such as a skull or a cranium, may be indifferent in a given sentence, but one form or the other will be related to occurrence in discourses about physical anthropology or graveyards.

The three main types of figures and images that I shall try to set up are simple transfers, or tropes (as in the paragraph above), analogies, and icons. Almost paradoxically, the simplest of these types, the trope, is the one that causes the most trouble. To define the term more exactly, we can say that a trope is the use of a term drawn from one contextual set (cooccurrence set) in another contextual, or cooccurrence set. Probably the *locus classicus* for the discussion of tropes is the expression "the ship plows the waves."[10] Whether or not this is to be taken as a realized image, it is pretty certainly a genuine trope. The problem of recognizing a trope—or perhaps one of the problems— is in recognizing the primary sense of the term; that is, whether a transfer has taken place and, if so, in what direction. *Plow* as a verb is an unusually clear case, since the existence of *plow* (noun) makes it seem quite reasonable to say that the primary meaning of *plow* (verb) is to move like a *plow* (noun). Such a statement is, of course, quite independent of any etymological evidence showing the noun or the verb to have been the earlier form of the word. In other suspected transfers, evidence of a different nature can sometimes be brought to bear. For instance, if we hear the expression "an arm of the sea," for *inlet*, we can be reasonably sure that "arm of the sea" is a transfer from "arm of a human being." The reason, of course, is the truism that mankind observes the world from himself and his own body outward, not outward first and himself second. But in plenty of examples of possible tropes we cannot be sure that a transfer has taken place, let alone the direction of it. Such a situation is "roar of the wind"; I have heard the occasional suggestion that this is a transfer from some such context as "roar of a lion."[11] We have no means, in such a phrase, of determining that one or the other context is primary, and we are forced, therefore, to say that *roar* is simply the word for a certain kind of noise, equally appropriate whether the noisemaker is the wind, a lion, or a motorcycle. The problem is something that has long been common knowledge. It is the problem of *dead metaphors*. The term is not a very good one, since, strictly speaking, it is the problem of empty tropes rather than of metaphors. Yet the term *dead metaphor* (itself a trope) has its own excellence, since it indicates that a phrase like "the roar of the wind" might once have been a trope of some vividness, though one from which the meaning has been drained over a period of time. We can be sure that "roar of the wind" is dead, in short, because we cannot be sure of an original meaning from which there has been a transfer; we cannot, indeed, be sure that it was ever a trope at all.

In order to deal with constructions like "the ship plows the waves" and "the roar of the wind," we can call on a general principle in semantics, the so-called Joos law. This is the formulation that, in arriving at the meaning of an unknown term in a context where the rest is known, the best meaning is that which contributes least to the sum total of meaning of the whole context. That is, to give an example, a sentence such as "he stirred his tea with a silver *plackswer*," is more likely to contain a synonym for *spoon* than for *chafing dish*. The formulation is sometimes objected to for reasons that we will mention as we go on, but at least in practical situations all of us follow the rule in interpreting strange items, even though we may not do so fully consciously.[12]

I can now add a corollary to the Joos law, which is that, when a meaning suggested by a narrower context is in conflict with one suggested by a wider context, it is the wider context which takes precedence. A case in point is the story of the Oxford students in a dining hall who rioted when a reader came to the phrase "Watery bier" in *Lycidas*. The interpretation they gave is ludicrous because it is based on a context of only two words and is quite out of keeping with the context found in the rest of the sentence and in the surrounding sentences. The point need not be labored but is at least necessary before I go on to a second corollary. This corollary is that it is only an unknown term that is without exception translated in the minimal Joos-law fashion. Suppose that the term is one like *plow*, fully known to all native speakers of English. In such circumstances, a corollary can be formulated to read that, if such a term in a given context is subjected to examination, it is then translated as having all the elements of meaning that can be derived from all other contexts in which the term is found, as long as these other-context sememes do not radically change the context under examination. Thus one context that contains sememes which would automatically be rejected in interpreting "the ship plows the waves" would be that from *Antony and Cleopatra*, "He ploughed her and she cropt,"[13] since the notion of impregnation would very radically change the context of ship and waves. That is, an analyst whose attention has been called to a passage in need of interpretation can be expected to make a mental review of all the contexts in which the questioned term can be found, interpret each in accord with the Joos law, and then apply the results to the passage under examination, in terms not of a strict Joos-law minimalizing process but, rather, of the maximum number of sememes not contradicted by the examined passage. Thus, for a conscious analyst, the Joos law is greatly modified in application when the questioned term is known from other contexts.

Yet we all know that tropes do lose meaning. Characteristically they are fresh and striking in a first use yet soon wear out. John Donne's "Till age snow white haires on thee," in *Song,*[14] is fresh, but the commoner "snowy head" is far less vivid. That is, it must always be remembered that it is not the normal communication situation for hearer or reader to examine messages closely. If communication is to succeed in its purpose, the desired modifications of conduct which the sentence or sentences as a whole are intended to produce must be understood quickly and the response given quickly if social interaction is to continue normally. Under such circumstances, then, it must be supposed that it is inevitable that the form and content of most utterances will not be subjected to close examination and that it is not merely the result of communicational laziness that this should be so. It is, however, precisely in literature that this sort of close examination we have been describing takes place, since a basic characteristic of literature is that it is preserved in permanent form and is regarded as more important than casual utterance, so that it becomes the proper subject for careful study.

It may, therefore, be worthwhile to reconstruct in an informal fashion the interpretation that an analyst might give to "the ship plows the waves." Specimen, though hypothetical, contexts for comparison might be the following:

1. The plow moved across the field in a straight line.
2. The plow dug a furrow, leaving a trench behind it.
3. The oxen dragged the plow across the field.
4. The plowman walked behind the plow, guiding it.

In (1) *plow* as a verb contrasts with *meander*—that is, a plow moves toward an invariant and purposeful goal. In (2) a plow moves across a surface but with penetration and disturbance, so that *plow* (verb) contrasts with *glide* on the one hand and with undersurface swimming on the other. These elements of meaning would then, in all probability, be given to *plow* in the examined sentence, though neither of the elements of meaning in (3) (dragged by a preceding source of motive power) nor in (4) (guided by a steersman walking behind) would be accepted.

It is noteworthy that in previous discussions, most literary critics and many linguists have insisted that this sort of meaning, which is the result of analysis, must be ascribed to literary tropes and that to deny it is narrowly antiaesthetic. I confess that my own views have changed somewhat with the passing of time. I should now say that the comparison-meaning of a trope is always potentially present and becomes real whenever the analysis is performed. It is subjective, however, to the extent that it is not possible to predict how much of the potential meaning will be discovered by any individual reader. Yet to say that it is potential and partially subjective is not to say that it is in any sense unreal when the comparison has been made. The meaning that is the result of comparison becomes illusory only if the student imports a meaning that is contradicted by the context or is without support in the context, as he might if he insisted that the phosphorescence of a ship's wake made a permanent track like a furrow so that an additional parallel would have to be added to *plow* (verb) in our original sentence.

We can say a number of other things about tropes. First, a very important fact is that a trope always rests on an undeveloped analogy; tropes contain a vehicle and tenor, to use the traditional terminology, as well as do analogies. It is therefore always possible for a reader to develop the analogy and thus restore the trope, which may for most readers be dead. That is, a reader who sees some commonplace trope like "That snake Mary" may actually compare the characteristics that belong to the girl and a snake to create a vivid pair of images. I believe that the act of comparison is more important than special, individual experience of the objects made use of in both halves of the trope, in spite of the views of many critics.[15] That is, if the reader has a vivid experience of snakes, he may create a very lively mental image of a serpent, but it does not follow that he necessarily creates an equally vivid image of Mary.

Further, the acts of comparison that revivify an empty trope are individual and subjective; therefore, they are quite unpredictable. Many students would argue that, subjective or not, they represent the reality of the trope and that whether or not a trope is empty varies solipsistically with every user of the language. As I have said a good many times, such a view is a counsel of despair. I believe, therefore, that the reality of a trope does not lie in the individual reader's mind but in a match between the reader's internal reaction and the total structure of the text before him. That reader's reaction is the best— not absolutely right but simply better than others—which gives the most exact match. Since the exactness of match can be investigated by experimenting with various reactions compared with the text, judgment is possible, and without judgment neither criticism nor analysis would be possible.

We find, in the other direction, a situation in which we can be sure that a trope is fully vivid, when it occurs in a cluster of other tropes, or of particularly concrete terms. An interesting example is from the Middle English poem *Sir Gawain and the Green Knight*, line 800. The line contains the word "poudred" (i.e., "powdered") referring to towers and pinnacles clustering thickly on a castle. Translators have often rendered it merely "scattered" or "placed about," but the whole passage is characterized by vividly concrete terms, many of them tropes. A better translation, then, would seem to be Modern English *powdered*, taking the occurrence as a living trope, not an empty figure.[16]

A final statement about tropes is that in one situation, a trope can be safely interpreted as empty; the Aristotelian "the arrow flew" is the example. The phrase contains no mention of anything that would justify setting up an analogy, such as the arrow is to the air as a bird is to the air. To bring in a comparison with a bird is to make use of an unneeded hypothesis. Also, we can by no means be sure that a transfer has taken place at all. The meaning of *fly* does not have to be taken to be "moves as birds move." It can perfectly well be taken to mean "moves as arrows, spears, birds, butterflies, and even airplanes move."

I have spent this long on tropes because they are more difficult to interpret than other figures and because the principles of interpretation have not (to my knowledge) been stated explicitly anywhere. Actually, however, tropes are the least interesting of literary and stylistic figures and are least effective in bringing richness of meaning and vividness of imagery. They are also nearest to the basic and normal uses of language. Every use of a linguistic item is an application of the term to a new situation, necessarily at least a tiny bit different from all others in the past. Thus each use of a linguistic item is in some sense a transfer, though obviously one in which the element of newness is minimal and easily disregarded.[17]

Our next figure is the type for which I have adopted the name *icon*. An icon is a direct description in which words are employed in their ordinary senses, without transfer and without setting up an analogical type of comparison. To give an extremely simple example, the following sentence is an icon in this sense: John was *short, fat,* and *bald.* The term *icon* is used because, granted the way in which language represents the nonlinguistic world, a natural resemblance exists between the set of sememes gathered together and the object toward which they are directed. We find, then, a situation not unlike that in which the colors employed by a painter form a natural representation of his subject, also something for which the term *icon* is used. Icons have not generally been included among the enumerations of figures of speech and, in discussions of imagery, have usually been called simply descriptions.

Two observations can be made here about icons. First, they are never covert, as we shall see analogies may be. If, in fact, an icon describes a house (as Poe does) in such a way that the description suggests a man, then the description ceases to be an icon and becomes an analogy. Next, icons rather generally leave little doubt that they are real—that is, that they form a genuine part of the design of the utterance. It is, usually at least, possible to check the parts of an icon against the surrounding context, thus determining their fit with the total design. Only in case a possible icon has been used to the point at which it becomes a cliché which is used as a whole, without attention to the meaning of its parts, would we be dealing with an icon whose meaning has been lost. A typical cliché of the sort I have in mind is a phrase like "dull, sickening thud." If one says, for instance, that "the book hit the floor with a dull, sickening thud," we could be reasonably sure that the pseudoicon was merely a cliché, since it does not fit with something relatively hard like a book. I shall return to the matter of discrimination between genuine and merely empty icons after I have taken up the next and last type of figure, the analogy.

Icons, like analogies, may be short like the simple example I have given or be extended, perhaps as far as the total of a story or an essay. It thus becomes possible to speak of the whole of a story or an essay as iconic or analogic in style. A realistic story, such as *Robinson Crusoe*, is iconic, whereas (to name a well-marked example) any story by Franz Kafka is analogic. It is of course true that stories, or even single passages, may show both analogic or iconic characteristics, as we shall see in detail later. It is also true that an icon— again like an analogy—does not have to be directed toward description alone. Icons can perfectly well be models of action and so be narrative in form instead of descriptive.

An icon is, by very definition, a model of either an object or an event. The fact that it is a model makes the kind of criticism commonly directed toward an icon understandable and fits it into a general scheme of criticism. When we say that an extended icon—perhaps a love story—is not true to life, we are saying that the model does not fit the object, just as we would criticize an architectural model which was out of proportion or which left out, or added, details so as not to be in proper relation to the object modeled.

We can now pass to my last type of figure, the analogy. In one sense, nothing is very new in saying that the analogy is a general type of metaphor and simile. Recognition of the general quality of analogy in most metaphors is not infrequently pointed out, as when Miss Brooke-Rose takes Aristotle to task for making analogies a separate type of metaphor, since she finds that all metaphors contain analogies. I will, however, be somewhat more rigorous than is usual and insist that there must be at least four terms in anything that is to be called an analogy—that is, the form must be that of A is to B as C is to D. As we shall see, however, there are analogies in which the four terms, though presumably present, are left undefined. A typical, fully developed analogy, where all four parts are clearly stated and identified is the first verse of Edgar Allan Poe's *To Helen*:

> Helen, thy beauty is to me
> Like those Nicéan barks of yore,
> That gently, o'er a perfumed sea,
> The weary, way-worn wanderer bore
> To his own native shore.[19]

That is, the basic analogy is that Helen's beauty is to the speaker as Nicéan bark is to the wanderer. It is interesting, though perhaps not important, that no one seems to know exactly what a Nicéan bark is; the analogy works independently of the identification. The bark is simply something vaguely classical that brings wanderers home.

More commonly an analogy does not mention all the parts. Instead, it leaves one unidentified, so that the reader is expected to fill it in. A typical example is again from Poe. In the first paragraph of *The Fall of the House of Usher* Poe speaks of the front of the house as having "vacant eye-like windows." That is, windows are to the house as eyes are to *X*—an easily supplied term, namely, *face*. Even the *Helen* analogy given above actually has an unsupplied term, though the unsupplied term is beyond the necessary minimum of four. The analogy contains six terms, one of which is left unnamed. If we give them in a different order we get: Bark is to wanderer is to return as Helen's beauty is to speaker is to spiritual return. The term *return* in the second half of the analogy is not specifically mentioned.

Oftentimes an analogy reveals more clearly how it works when it is less than fully successful. What seems to me the worst analogy in the whole of English poetry is to be found in a poem written by no less a poet than John Dryden, albeit in only his seventeenth year. The poem is *Upon the Death of Lord Hastings*. The occasion for the remarkable analogy is the death of Hastings from smallpox

> Each little pimple had a tear in it,
> To wail the fault its rising did commit;[20]

That is, discharge is to pustule is to rising as tears are to eyes are to sorrow for Hastings's death. Surely no other poet has managed to compare men to pimples, and surely Dryden would not have done so had he realized where his analogy was taking him.

At this point, also, we can make another observation about analogies. They frequently operate, as this one does, by transfer of a vocabulary item from one of the double targets of comparison to the other. In this case, *tear* has been transferred from the context of sorrowful eyes to the context of disease. In this, of course, the analogy is very like a trope, since the process is exactly the same. The only difference is that in a genuine analogy we can be sure that both of the two targets are, in some sense, present in the design of the utterance, though with an analogy as repulsive as the one just quoted, it is probably necessary to say that the poet was not composing carefully. With a trope, on the other hand, we can be sure of only one of the two targets, so that we always have a danger of interpreting as if there were two. Suppose Dryden had merely said "the pustule wept." A conservative interpretation, as I have tried to indicate earlier, would lead us merely to equate *tears* as the equivalent of *discharge*. Whether or not both pustules and eyes were clearly visualized in the mind of the poet would in that case have remained unknowable, in the absence of any evidence other than the one item under consideration.

Lest one should think that repulsive analogies are the sole property of seventeenth-century verse, I can add another, which is from a bit of magazine verse by a contemporary of some reputation, whom I will mercifully leave unidentified. The poet was speaking of a love affair and said "the night was a nest of your hair, filled with your eyes." I leave my readers to work out the details of the analogy for themselves. It would seem necessary as a result of such poetic monstrosities as I have quoted to suppose that the poet must have some sort of "deep structure machine," which constructs analogies for him which are suitable on a relatively narrow context, without the analogy rising to a point in consciousness where it can be examined to see whether it is suitable on a wider context.

I have been dealing with analogies which leave one term unidentified. It is not by any means necessary that one term be undefined, since the analogy may very well be explicit in all, or at least most, of its parts. Such an explicit analogy is that by Alice Meynell in *The Shepherdess*, though, since it is also true that it is a carefully extended analogy, we eventually come to likenesses that we must supply for ourselves. I will not quote all of the poem.

> She walks—the lady of my delight—
> A shepherdess of sheep.
> Her flocks are thoughts . . .

That is, thoughts are to the lady as sheep are to the shepherdess. The poem is unusual only in that it is built around this single analogy, extended through all three verses, so that we continue to such lines as:

> She holds her little thoughts in sight,
> Though gay they run and leap.[21]

One of the distinctions of which critics have been well aware is that between the extended analogy, as in the poem just quoted, and the minimal analogy like the "eye-like windows" of Poe. It is certainly true that we find a difference in effect between an explicit analogy thus relentlessly pursued and the
relatively light and passing use of *eyes* and *windows* from Poe's first paragraph. In traditional criticism of imagery, however, this distinction is more or
less obscured by being crossed with others, so that it may be worthwhile to
reclassify from a different point of view. One of the oldest distinctions, of
course, is that between metaphor and simile. I believe that it is perhaps more
revealing to speak, instead, of overt, implied, and covert analogies. An analogy is overt if the speaker uses any one of the several grammatical forms which
states that a comparison is occurring. These may be in the shape of A is like B
or an A makes a B or A has the characteristics of B. In general, however, the
shape A is B does not necessarily constitute an overt analogy, since such a
statement as "John is an old fox" is either a trope or a statement which was
once a trope but has lost content. That is, "old fox," by virtue of having
become widely current, can be said to be no more than an equivalent of "clev-
er, tricky man." When we have such a statement as Thomas Campion's

> There is a garden in her face
> Where roses and white lilies grow,[22]

the result is a clearly recognizable analogy, not because of the occurrence of
the copula, which unites face and garden, but because of the implied constituents: roses and lilies are to a garden as rosy color and white color are to a face.

When an analogy is complete or, even more, when it is extended beyond
the necessary four terms, it makes little difference whether it is marked by
some statement of comparison. If we have an extended analogy for lovers'
souls, as in Donne,

> . . . they are two so
>   As stiffe twin compasses are two,
> Thy soule the fixt foot, makes no show
> To move, but doth, if th'other doe,[23]

it will surely make no difference to the total effect (barring metrical form) if
we should change the first partial line to read "lovers' souls are like stiff twin
compasses." The implied cluster of correspondences produces the effect,
whether they are labeled for us or not.

I find only one situation in which the use of a specific label of comparison
produces an effect differing from that which occurs with an analogy not so
labeled. We have seen that the statement "John is an old fox" is subject to

meaning loss and may therefore be no more than a dead trope. If, however, we have a statement of comparison, the normal implication is that the speaker has made a statement which must be believed. That is, a simile forces the reader to hunt for correspondences between vehicle and tenor, even when they are not mentioned, or when the one set does not obviously correspond to the other. The first type—the undeveloped simile—can be found in the songwriter's line "A pretty girl is like a melody," and the second in the much discussed line from Eliot:

> When the evening is spread out against the sky
> Like a patient etherized upon a table;[24]

Not that the figure from Eliot may not have dramatic appropriateness. Considered in itself, however, there is certainly difficulty in finding the expected points of correspondence. With all figures of the A is like B type, however, the occurrence of the label of comparison forces the reader or hearer to hunt for some analogical structure which will fulfill the pattern.

An implied analogy is one in which the form is A has characteristics x, y, and z; B has characteristics x', y', and z', but the reader is left to observe that the pattern for A is compared to that for B. A perfect example is the little poem *Light*, by F. W. Bourdillon.

> The night has a thousand eyes,
> The day but one,
> Yet the light of a bright world dies
> With the dying sun.
>
> The mind has a thousand eyes,
> And the heart but one;
> Yet the light of a whole life dies
> When love is done.[25]

Or, perhaps, the even better known Longfellow poem *The Arrow and the Song*. It is a rather obvious comment that the occurrence of grammatical parallelism, as with Bourdillon, greatly heightens the explicitness of the analogy.

Some of the most interesting analogies are of the covert sort, and often a covert analogy is the subject of considerable uncertainty and controversy. A covert analogy exists when an object or event is described apparently as an icon and no more, but on a second level of reading it can be discovered that the characteristics given in the icon also fit a second object or event. If, in turn, correspondence with the second object fits with the larger context in which the passage is found, we have, then, good reason for supposing that the analogy is real.

An excellent example of a covert analogy, which also is one which is accepted by all critics and all ordinary readers, is found in the description of Roderick Usher's painting in Poe's story:

> One of the phantasmagoric conceptions of my friend, partaking not so rigidly of the spirit of abstraction, may be shadowed forth, although feebly, in words. A small picture presented the interior of an immensely long and rectangular vault or tunnel, with low walls, smooth, white, and without interruption or device. Certain accessory points of the design served well to convey the idea that this excavation lay at an exceeding depth below the surface of the earth. No outlet was observed in any portion of its vast extent, and no torch or other artificial source of light was discernible; yet a flood of intense rays rolled throughout, and bathed the whole in a ghastly and inappropriate splendor.[26]

The scene is clearly meant to represent the interior of a coffin, buried but left vacant. The parallels to a coffin are at least six in number—the chamber is long and narrow; it has low walls; the walls are smooth and bare; the chamber is underground; there is no outlet; there is no source of light. The six parallels are enough to establish the analogy, even though they do not contain a parallel in order of characteristics, which is usually the clinching detail in the establishment of parallels.

In an essay later in this volume I have written of the probabilities involved in interpretation of a cluster of correspondences such as we have here. I shall not anticipate by going into details at this point, but it is possible to say that the probability of a correspondence being meaningful is at least doubled with the addition of every new parallel item. If there are six parallel items, as in this description of the picture-coffin, the number of parallels puts the general correspondence well over the threshold of parallel by design rather than by chance. There seems no reason, then, for anyone to argue that Poe's analogy is anything other than meaningful.[27]

It is interesting, on the other hand, that, considered simply as an icon—a description of a picture and nothing more—Poe's paragraph is something of a failure. We are told that it is a small picture and that it represents "the interior of . . . a vault." The suggestion is that the interior of the vault fills the whole of the canvas. We are next told that "certain accessory points of the design served well" to represent the vault as at a vast depth below the surface of the earth. The only way that this could be done is by representing the earth or a portion of it in cross section, which is ruled out by the apparent fact that the picture of the vault occupies the whole canvas. Also, we are told that there is neither outlet nor source of light. Yet, if a chamber is represented from inside, as this one is, any human observer will necessarily assume that the outlet and source of light are both behind him. Poe's mystery evaporates on examination. The paragraph is, then, an interesting example of the way in which a single passage serves as both icon and analogy. Indeed, in any analogy there must always be both an iconic and an analogic level, since otherwise we will not have the necessary vehicle and tenor for a comparison. It is also an interesting example of the way in which criticism can be directed toward an icon. This one is imperfect because its parts do not correspond with the known and culturally shared facts which the icon is supposed to represent.

A second way in which the counting of correspondences has some relevance in dealing with icons is that the number of correspondences in a cluster has a direct bearing on the vividness of the imagery. When we have a group of correspondences, the reader's reaction is to be convinced that the author was drawing from an event actually experienced, or an object seen. If correspondences are only minimal, we are not thus convinced, and we do not ourselves share the realization of the image with the same sharpness. O. Henry in *The Furnished Room* gives an extended description of the contents of a typical room in a New York rooming house. Not all of it is equally successful, but a passage which most readers remember is the following: "The tiny fingerprints on the wall spoke of little prisoners trying to feel their way to sun and air. A splattered stain, raying like the shadow of a bursting bomb, witnessed where a hurled glass or bottle had splintered with its contents against the wall. Across the pier glass had been scrawled with a diamond in staggering letters the name 'Marie.'" Fingerprints, stain, and name add up to an effective cluster. It is in strong contrast with another part of the description of the room which employs a hastily drawn analogy and a series of modifiers which do not form correspondences with the object modeled but merely say that the speaker disapproves: "The furnished room received its latest guest with a first glow of pseudo-hospitality, a hectic, haggard, perfunctory welcome like the specious smile of a demirep."[28]

If we pass now to the larger relations of icons and analogies, it should be reasonably clear that (as we have already said) the kind of style that is usually called realistic is essentially an iconic style. That which is called figurative is often essentially tropic, and I believe that which is characterized by frequent and extended use of analogies is what we generally call symbolist. Note, for instance, the structured analogies between black lamb and white lamb, between black boy and white boy, and between chimney sweep and village child in William Blake's *Songs*, one of the most striking examples of a deeply symbolist style that I know. Notice also that a recognizable, but only slightly developed, genre in our culture presents a recognizable icon, composed of parts all of which are natural and correspond with experience, though the sum total is strange. The result is that the reader inevitably hunts for an analogy which would explain the strangeness away by making it meaningful. A typical example of such a piece is Robert Frost's poem *The Draft Horse*, where a pair of people are said to be riding through a dark and endless grove, with a lantern that does not burn, and are suddenly stopped by a man who without apparent reason stabs the horse and forces the travelers to walk the rest of the way.[29] The poem was once made the subject of a sort of quiz program for a group of students, critics, and teachers of literature, who did not by any means agree on what the analogy was, though it was perfectly plain that all of them were sure that there must be some analogy which explains the strangeness of the narrative. It is to be noted, at least in passing, that this type of narrative is not far from the type that has been developed as a major genre in one national literature, the Japanese haiku. The haiku gives an iconic representation of an event or an object with a maximum of brevity, so that the icon seems pointless unless the reader supplies an analogy for himself. An example is this from the writings of the famous poet Matsuo Bashō:

> With the scent of plums
> on the mountain road—suddenly
> sunrise comes![30]

The poem is pointless unless we see in the suddenly perceived scent of blossoms a promise of the whiteness of the blossoms themselves like the sudden sunrise.

A much more important genre in our culture, into which the unexplained icon form easily shades, is that of near-allegory. Almost any of the stories of Kafka, whether we choose *The Country Doctor*, *The Hunger Artist*, or *In the Penal Colony*, are icons which are extremely realistic in detail though very strange in sum total. For all of them, analogies, though not always easy to identify, are available. Always the analogies make the stories meaningful, as does Austin Warren's explanation of *In the Penal Colony* as an analogy for the breakdown of traditional views of sin and punishment under modern conditions.[31] Finally, setting up analogy as one of the basic types of linguistic and literary expression enables us to define the genre of allegory with increased ease. An allegory is an extended analogy, arranged in narrative, in which nonhuman objects are personified and in which label-names are employed. It is to be distinguished from a *roman à clef* in that the latter is a similar analogy but one in which there is a human parallel for human persons and events. An allegory, of course, may be a member of both types as is *The Faerie Queene*. It is certainly true that a student may list the characteristics of allegory much more extensively than those I have enumerated here, but, as definition rather than description, I believe that those I have given are sufficient.

To summarize, I believe that the basic types of figure, image, and semantic construct, stylistically considered, are three: the trope, or transferred vocabulary item, the icon, and the analogy. The first type is not an image which the reader or hearer is forced to share. It is a potential image only. A trope can be supposed to be an effective image when it fits with the total structure of the text, and it can be rejected as empty when it does not so fit or when it has been commonly associated with the items with which it is found cooccurring, as in "dull, sickening thud."

An icon is a direct representation of an object or an event, with linguistic items employed in their ordinary senses. An analogy is a sort of double model in which the first target is presented iconically and the second may be presented as a parallel to the first. In the implied type of analogy, however, both types are presented iconically. Analogies may be divided into clustered and ordered correspondences, on the one hand, and by a different and overlapping classification into overt, implied, and covert correspondences, on the other. I should, incidentally, prefer these types of classification to the sort so elaborately given by Miss Brooke-Rose, since I do not believe that any marked difference of effect is produced by analogies which employ (to name one example of her classification) a nominal as against a verbal parallel—provided only that the parallel is genuinely present. I should, perhaps, also say that the order of presentation which I have chosen—trope, icon, and analogy—is not the only one which might have been used. Tropes are essentially potential and undeveloped analogies and so might have been treated together with them. I chose the order given so as to move from simple to more complex and from uncertain to certain.

I can conclude with an oblique reference to language universals, which are things that currently excite linguists. Universals may be parallel to the forms of logic and may indeed be logically derived, though many scholars are skeptical. It is certain, however, that there are universals for which the evidence is empirical, because these phenomena have been observed to occur in such numerous and widely different languages and communities that they can with reasonable safety be supposed to be universal. I believe the three types of approaches to conveyance of meaning found in tropes, icons, and analogies which I have presented are universals, but in the field of stylistics, not linguistics. The late J. R. Firth wrote a stimulating and fruitful essay in which he described at length the importance of contexts and collocations in conveying meaning. The title was *Modes of Meaning*.[32] I may be pardoned for borrowing his title for use in an essay which complements rather than contradicts his and which also complements the studies of the current school of linguistic universalists. My three types are also modes of meaning, and I believe they are the fundamental universal and inescapable modes of meaning in stylistics.

Chapter Seven
Imagery and Meaning: A Passage from
Lycidas and a Poem by Blake

A number of years before writing this essay I attempted to defend two lines by William Blake against the possible charge that they contained a mixed metaphor.[1] The lines were:

And the hapless Soldier's sigh
Runs in blood down Palace walls.

Sighs do not literally run in blood. I was able, however, to show that the lines belonged to an integrated structure of analogies, which fully justified the falsification of literal fact. Contrariwise, after the justification, I found myself troubled by a passage from *Lycidas* which is generally admired but which I could not accept. The Milton passage is:

Blind mouthes! that scarce themselves know how to hold
A Sheep-hook, or have learn'd ought els the least
That to the faithful Herdmans art belongs![2]

I should like to return to both passages and, indeed, to take up the Blake poem entire, since it offers a number of problems in meaning. The Blake poem, furthermore, is a specially good object of study, since Blake's text is available in unusually full form. We thus find two avenues of investigation of meaning: textual variants and drafts and the structure of imagery. I believe, therefore, that discussion of the poem should offer a number of points of method, perhaps even of general principles, which should be useful in the evaluation of imagery and, even more so, in the recovery of meaning.

First, for the Milton passage. All scholars are acquainted with the spirited defense of it made over a century ago by John Ruskin, which has never been questioned to my knowledge. It would seem to constitute the still orthodox attitude toward the passage, since it is frequently quoted or paraphrased,[3]

Note: This essay was originally published in *Texas Studies in Literature and Language* 11 (1969): 1093–1105, under the title "Imagery and Meaning: A Passage from Milton, and from Blake." Since publication it has passed under the editorial eye and pen of Martin Joos, and a considerable revision has resulted from his suggestions. Needless to say, I am grateful to him.

though often so briefly as to suggest that its source is unknown and that its substance is regarded as unquestioned fact unnecessary of defense like a statement that the earth is round. The Ruskin passage is worth quoting entire:

> . . . a broken metaphor, one might think, careless and unscholarly.
>
> Not so; its very audacity and pithiness are intended to make us look close at the phrase and remember it. These two monosyllables express the precisely accurate contraries of right character in the two great offices of the Church—those of the Bishop and the pastor.
>
> A "bishop" means "a person who sees."
>
> A "pastor" means "a person who feeds."
>
> The most unbishoply character a man can have is, therefore, to be blind.
>
> The most unpastoral is, instead of feeding, to want to be fed,—to be a mouth.
>
> Take the two reverses together, and you have "blind mouthes."[4]

Two related, but different, questions arise in coming to a conclusion about the Ruskin hypothesis. The first of these is to decide, if we can, whether or not it is probable that Milton had a reference to bishops in mind as he wrote the passage as well as to pastors, who are quite obviously present, being inherent in the poet's statements about sheep and shepherds. I cannot, of course, really measure the probabilities that "blind" refers to bishops and "mouthes" to pastors, though it is striking that the two should be found together—more so than if they had been found widely separated. Yet, striking as the juxtaposition is, it is surely not beyond the reach of chance. I therefore think it necessary to bring in another point of method. The passage undoubtedly refers to the secular clergy, the parish priests. These can easily be described as unseeing and selfish without reference to any other level of the ecclesiastical hierarchy. In short, the reference to bishops is an unnecessary supposition and, so, is to be rejected on the grounds of parsimony of hypotheses.

The second question is whether "blind mouthes" is effective, irrespective of whether it was created by chance or intention. The passage is certainly altogether negative, since "blind" applied to "mouthes" is the equivalent of saying that mouths are sightless because they are eyeless, as mouths normally are. Further, the mouth does not normally hold a sheephook. Such a negative approach has always, perhaps irrelevantly, reminded me of the proverbial English schoolboy's comment that "large pennies has saved many lives by not a-swallowing of 'em." More seriously, it is a general principle that negative imagery does not work negatively. Thus one could not successfully describe the quiet of the deep woods by listing all the city noises which were not present. The result would be to produce a vivid impression of noise, not of silence. Similarly, in this passage, "blind mouthes" also works in reverse to give the incongruous impression of mouths with eyes in them, and "scarce themselves know how to hold/A Sheep-hook" also conjures up the image of a hook carried in the mouth as by some monstrous kind of sheepdog. The principle of the ineffectiveness of negative imagery—by no means a new one—is surely borne out here, and the image must be regarded as unfortunate. Why, then, did Ruskin, astute and learned critic that he was, praise the line? I think his praise is due to one of the oldest temptations in literary study. Whenever a poem is one that we admire greatly in its sum total, it is hard not to be tempted to explain away details in it that might be thought blemishes if they occurred in less-admirable works. One need only look at the tortured comments of Shakespeareans on Hamlet's taking "armes against a Sea of troubles" to see the tendency at work in extreme form.[5] Surely it is preferable to admit that great poetry often contains faults, since nothing is perfect in an imperfect world. To insist that all blemishes can be justified is to open the way to vitiating inconsistency in all our analyses. A word might also be added about the many critics and students who have accepted the Ruskin pronouncement and think of "blind mouthes" as a successful image. Insofar as they are not submitting to the same temptation that overcame Ruskin, they are, I think, reacting not to the image alone but to the combination of the image and the Ruskin explanation, which then makes of the image a successful and very compressed comment. Such a reaction is justified enough—*de gustibus non est disputandum,* of course—but it is still true that it is worth any scholar's while to know whether he is reacting to the text alone, to the footnotes, or to a combination of both. Incidentally, I have long suspected that the passage contains a covert reference to a leech, the one creature that could be best described as a "blind mouth" and which would be a quite appropriate symbol for a rapacious clergyman.[6] I cannot prove the guess, certainly, but leeches were common enough on account of their use in medicine and so would have been a vivid part of Milton's experience.

Turning now to Blake, I shall begin by quoting the poem entire, followed by the draft of it found in Blake's notebook.

LONDON

I wander thro' each charter'd street,
Near where the charter'd Thames does flow,
And mark in every face I meet
Marks of weakness, marks of woe.

In every cry of every Man,
In every Infant's cry of fear,
In every voice, in every ban,
The mind-forg'd manacles I hear.

How the Chimney-sweeper's cry
Every black'ning Church appalls;
And the hapless Soldier's sigh
Runs in blood down Palace walls.

But most thro' midnight streets I hear
How the youthful Harlot's curse
Blasts the new-born Infant's tear,
And blights with plagues the Marriage hearse.

The poem is number 16 in *Songs of Experience*. The draft follows:

LONDON
First draft of the poem with the same title in Songs of Experience . . .

I wander thro' each dirty street,
Near where the dirty Thames does flow,
And [see *del.*] mark in every face I meet
Marks of weakness, marks of woe.

In every cry of every man
In [every voice of every child *del.*]
    every infant's cry of fear
In every voice, in every ban
The [german *del.*] mind forg'd [links I hear *del.*]
                            manacles I hear.

[But most *del.*] How the chimney sweeper's cry
[Blackens o'er the churches' walls, *del.*]
Every black'ning church appalls,
And the hapless soldier's sigh
Runs in blood down palace walls.

[But most the midnight harlot's curse
From every dismal street I hear,
Weaves around the marriage hearse
And blasts the new born infant's tear. *del.*]

But most [from every *del.*] thro' wintry streets I hear
How the midnight harlot's curse
Blasts the new born infant's tear,
And [hangs *del.*] smites with plagues the marriage hearse.

But most the shrieks of youth I hear
But most thro' midnight & . . . .
How the youthful . . .[7]

Evidence for understanding the imagery and language of the poem can be drawn from several areas, of increasing particularity and nearness to the text itself. The most distant area is the general background which includes knowledge of Blake's times and of the ideas and attitudes made use of.[8] It also includes knowledge of the language of Blake's day, though it is evident that, almost solely, knowledge of vocabulary is relevant. The only detail that falls outside vocabulary is the very tiny syntactic detail that Blake could use the verbal phrase "does flow" as a merely convenient metrical filler—a phrasal type and usage amply attested in Elizabethan times (as in Shakespeare's line from Ariel's song, which employs the simple verb and the phrase side by side, *"There I couch when owles do crie"*)[9] which is found throughout the eighteenth century but is scarcely possible today. Just as with ideas, events, and language, it is necessary to explore not only the general usage of the time but also Blake's own habits. Thus, in vocabulary, it is possible to compare usage in this poem with other uses in Blake's writings.

When we have passed from the background area, we come to that of stylistics, which also has an area of greater generality, and one restricted to the poem itself. The more general area is the study of the successive drafts of the poem, and the narrower one is the study of the final form of the text for what structural patterns and relationships it may reveal.[10]   We can begin with the background, taking it up generally first, though when we come to consider specific items from the poem, we shall return to background material as it is needed. Two institutions, or practices, of the time need comment, since one of them is largely forgotten and the other, fortunately, considerably modified. The first of these is the practice of using children to crawl through the multitudinous flues of ancient buildings to remove the soot, which was an ever-present danger of fire. The chimney sweeps were virtual slaves under the outworn apprentice system inherited from the Middle Ages. They were dirty, ill fed, and continuously exposed to danger of suffocation. Their state is well suggested in that "Porter's law" in 1788 decreed that the "climbing boys" should not be apprenticed before the age of eight, should have their heads shaved, be bathed once a week, and not be compelled to crawl into lighted flues.[11] It is an ironical comment that, in spite of such humanitarian laws, the practice of using sweeps did not disappear until flues were lined with fireproof brick. The second great social evil all too well known to us, though in a lessened form, is prostitution. The uprooting of a once rural population and its concentration in expanding and ill-regulated cities brought not only slums but also vast human misery and brutalization. Blake was far different from his contemporaries in insisting on the relation between ideas of respectability then current and exploitation of poor women.[12]

The sources of Blake's ideas—revolutionary, antiindustrial, and, in modern terms, more nearly anarchistic than communistic—have been well summarized by Mark Schorer, who says, "The lines echo with Paine on monopoly, Godwin on child labor, Mary Wollstonecraft on marriage."[13] Yet, while it is important to place Blake in his proper position in the history of social thought, it is not necessary to explore this formative reading in detail, since the ideas are still fully familiar to a modern reader. We can, then, pass to a consideration of specific vocabulary items from the poem, making use, as promised, of evidence from any area in which the evidence may be found.

The items we shall take up, in the order in which they are found in the poem, are *charter'd* (lines 1 and 2), *ban* (line 7), *appalls* (line 10), *curse* (line 14), and *Marriage hearse* (line 16).

In dealing with *charter'd*, we must first decide its identity. It is, so students have told me, sometimes described as a variant of *charted*. Such an identification is possible, though it should not be accepted without examination. Blake, as a Londoner, can be presumed to have spoken an "*r*-less" dialect, in which unstressed syllables containing an /r/ plus consonant, as in *charter'd*, would be indistinguishable from syllables not containing /r/. For Blake, *charter'd* and *charted* may well have been homonyms, so that uncertainty in spelling might have resulted. Confusion between words containing the letter *r* and those without it can be manifested in two ways. One is habitual omission of the letter in spelling, as was common with Keats.[14] A second is by insertion of the letter where it does not belong. A good example of such insertion is from a novel that I read shortly before writing this essay. One sentence from that book refers to John Paul Jones as having explored "the *unchartered* waters of Africa," and a second refers to the streets of eighteenth-century Paris as noisy with the clatter of "wooden shoes and *patterns*."[15] In each sentence the words called for are without the letter *r*, namely, *uncharted* and *pattens*. It is amusing that one of the words thus misspelled is the form under discussion at the moment.

Three instances of the word *charter'd* occur in Blake's lyrics, two from this poem and a third in which the Thames is referred to as having "the cheating waves of charter'd streams." All three are closely similar, and in all *charted* would be possible, since streets and rivers of London were surely mapped. Yet none of the three instances really rule out *chartered*, and, furthermore, no other words show an intrusion of *r*, as in the novel's *patterns*.

It is clear that *charter'd* is a word of disapproval, indicating a quality in streets and rivers that is bad. The immediate context speaks of *charter'd streets* as a region where people show "mind-forg'd manacles." The general context speaks of church, palace, and home as dirtied or diseased. In these contexts, as well as in others, the chief tool for recovery of meaning is, once again, the Joos law, which tells us to choose the least meaning for any unknown item and the maximal meaning for its context.[16]

The difficulty here is to find a possible meaning for *charter'd*, remembering that it is derived from a noun which earlier meant a legal document. The possible meaning we need must be one which will lead to one or other of the meanings suggested by the context and, then, enable us to decide between them.

One possibility of derivation is to assume development from *charter*, meaning a contract or instrument as is involved in sale of goods or land. The meaning could then be hypothesized as "bought and sold," extended, of course, to the Thames and the streets. It would mean something like "dirtied by commerce" and be in accord with the wider context of the poem. This is the meaning which I for long thought was the best hypothesis, though I no longer think so.

The second possibility is to derive the Blake usage from *charter* in the sense of a document guaranteeing liberties, in spite of the fact that Blake's term quite clearly means the reverse of the earlier sense. One stage of the development can be paralleled quite easily. *Chartered* in the sense of a document of liberties cannot, logically, be applied to a feature of the natural landscape, or geography, except by extension. This extension is evidenced by a quotation from a contemporary, who says, "What is Great Britain . . . but a charter'd isle [where all the cities] have their charters also." The bridge in meaning seems to be that indicated by David Erdman, who points out that Thomas Paine had condemned "charters and corporations" as cheating the people of true liberty,[17] much as laws intended to establish minimum wages tend to become laws for maximum wages as well.[18]

Blake's idiolectal lexicon supports the hypothesis that his use of *charter'd* indicates loss of liberty. Thus the whole of the little poem referred to above as containing the third occurrence of *charter'd* is:

Why should I care for the men of thames.
Or the cheating waves of charter'd streams,
Or shrink at the little blasts of fear
That the hireling blows into my ear?

Tho' born on the cheating banks of Thames,
Tho' his waters bathed my infant limbs,
The Ohio shall wash his stains from me:
I was born a slave, but I go to be free.[19]

It is clear from these verses not only that Thames is one of the *charter'd streams* but also that the *charter'd streams* are those that are associated with absence of the freedom that is found only on the banks of the Ohio. It is interesting that *charter'd* is also associated with *cheating*, which I should take as meaning "cheating of promised liberty," not as one commentator has taken it, "liberty to cheat."[20] Thus I find myself finally agreeing with those commentators who have taken *charter'd* to mean "deprived of liberty," rather than with those who have taken it to mean "soiled by commerce."[21] I should paraphrase the first four lines as follows: I wander through each enslaved street, near the enslaved Thames, and in every voice and ban of authority I hear "mind-forg'd manacles." Yet, even when we have reached a conclusion, two interesting methodological points can still be made. The first is that in the draft of the poem, quoted above, Blake first wrote *dirty*, the meaning which we have rejected. The point is small, perhaps, but it is certainly true that presence of a form in an earlier draft is not necessarily evidence for the meaning of the finally presented text. It must always be remembered that a poet quite frequently rejects a meaning and, therefore, that draft and final version can be quite different. In this instance I should suggest that Blake first wrote a form in keeping with the wider subject of the poem, dirt and soiling, then rejected it for the immediate context of loss of liberty. We shall see that instances occur in which a draft can indeed influence our interpretation of the final text, but at least I find it well to exercise caution.

The second methodological point has important bearing on the Joos law. In earlier use of it, I found it necessary to set up a corollary, namely, that in instances where a conflict arose between an interpretation suggested by a narrower context and one suggested by a wider context, the suggestion of the wider context was to be preferred. Here, however, it is the context of the first eight lines which suggests "enslaved," while the last eight lines suggest a general topic, "dirtied." It is the more immediate context which I have preferred. This preference leads me to set up a second corollary. In instances where a conflict between a meaning suggested by a vaguer context and one suggested by a more precise context arises, it is the more precise context whose suggestion is to be preferred. The collocation of "ban" (see the next paragraph) with "manacles," as well as "marks of weakness" and "cry of fear," quite specifically and precisely suggests loss of freedom. In the second part of the poem, buildings are specifically blackened, or figuratively reddened, while a symbolic "Marriage hearse" is infected. The suggestion of dirtiness is less consistent and less precise, which is why I have rejected it.

The next term on our list is *ban*. It suggests such uses as "crying the marriage banns" and meaning either "banish" or "curse" and, finally, "prohibition, or interdiction." The context clearly suggests that bans are something heard, since the collocation is with "voice" and "manacles," which are heard. The *OED* votes for "imprecation," perhaps because the glossator thought of prohibitions as more formal and less likely to have been given orally than is an imprecation. But the context gives us a little more, also. The "mind-forg'd manacles" are pretty clearly imposed on the Londoners by others, not by themselves. *Voice*, *ban*, and *manacles*, then, belong together and are the pronouncements of the cruel society which Blake is denouncing. Thus a consistent meaning for *ban* in this context is "prohibition," and the *OED* would have done well to quote the line under this gloss rather than under "imprecation." And if we take this meaning, we can quickly find support from the draft. In the draft we read the earliest version as "german links" rather than "mind-forg'd manacles." As Erdman has pointed out, the reference was to repressive measures which Blake blamed on George III.[22] The draft then suggests that *bans* are such things as prohibitions against seditious utterances, thought of by Blake as being orally pronounced (whether or not this was the actual case). It is unnecessary, I think, to see here, as Erdman does, a reference to curses written on palace walls.

In *appalls* (line 10) we have another one of the terms which is relatively easy to explain and on which the draft also casts some light. The situation is that church buildings are being blackened by soot, a dirtying which Blake poetically connects with the exploitation of chimney sweeps. The exploitation manifestly fails to horrify the Church, considered as an institution. Therefore the meaning suggested by the context is "casts a pall over." The meaning is possible for *appall*[23] and, though not recorded in dictionaries, is an understandable formation, related to *pall* (verb) in much the same way that *avow* is related to the verb *vow*. The *OED* does not, as just indicated, record any such meaning as "cast a pall over," for *appall*, though it does do so for *pall*. Further, it does say, "But *appall* cannot be separated from the simple *pall* v." The meaning "cast a pall over" is supported, however, by the draft line "Blackens o'er the churches' walls." It is noteworthy that in instances like

this a variant can be accepted as corroborative of the meaning which is probable for the final text. A draft cannot be accepted as evidence if its version contradicts the final text, since, as said, authors change their minds. Thus, for instance, line 13 has "midnight streets" in the final version. The two drafts
have "dismal street" and "wintry streets." It would be foolish to try to pick
either one of the drafts instead of the version finally chosen by Blake.

Another point of some interest can be made about the meaning of this term.
Hazard Adams seems to be of the opinion that *appalls* is a sort of pun on
blacken and *horrify*. He says, "With every cry heard the church becomes a
blacker spectre of itself . . . The church is once again a symbol of compla-
cency and blindness. It is 'appalled' at the conditions it observes in London
life, but its histrionic reaction is clearly hypocritical."[24] Such a view is
clearly in conflict with the law of least lexical contribution, since it is a view
that changes the meaning of the total context very greatly indeed. I think this
reading can be rejected also on the more general grounds of simplicity. The
meaning is adequately accounted for as "casts a pall over." It is therefore unnecessary to find a second semantic entity, especially one that is used with an
ironic reversal of its usual application.

Curse (line 14) is the simplest term deserving comment at all. Yet, once
again, *curse* gives a conflict in contextual meanings. Since the harlot's curse
blasts the infant's tear and blights marriage with plagues, it would be quite
possible to take *curse* in the sense of disease, though I know of only one commentator who has done so.[25] A wider context, however, establishes a different meaning. A sequence of chimney sweep's cry, soldier's sigh, and
harlot's curse establishes a pattern, and *curse* must therefore be an utterance,
an imprecation. It is a good instance of the first corollary of the law of least
lexical contribution that the wider context takes precedence over the narrower
one.

The last term is, in contrast to the preceding, very difficult indeed. It is
curious, also, that it has received little attention. Both *ban* and *charter'd* are
illustrated in the *OED* by lines from this poem, but the *OED*, and the commentators also, are silent on *marriage hearse* except for the briefest of comments, given without explanation. Two meanings are possible for *hearse*,
though neither is particularly appropriate to marriage. The current meaning is
"chariot in which a corpse is carried to the cemetery." An earlier meaning is
"bier," the bedlike platform on which a corpse rests. Both, of course, are
connected with death rather than marriage.

The first step is to decide which of these two meanings underlies its use
here. If we should blot out *hearse* and then ask a reader unacquainted with the
poem to fill in the resultant blank, he would almost certainly choose *bed*. It is
to be noted that Blake has directed his criticism toward religion, government,

and, finally, home. No very convenient symbol for home can be found except the marriage bed, since no building stands for it as buildings stand for the other two. Therefore, I think it more probable that the meaning of *hearse* in this line is "bier," or "bed of death," rather than "chariot for a corpse." Such a decision disposes, perhaps unfortunately, of some of the more vivid comments, such as that of Alfred Kazin that "the carriage that went to the church for a marriage ends at the grave as a hearse" and that of Sir Geoffrey Keynes that "the manacled mind converts the marriage bed into a sort of Black Maria or hearse."[26]

A more important question is how *Marriage hearse* fits into the sequence of church, palace, and home. In this series, I do not think that *hearse* fits perfectly. The first two symbols are soiled but are not destroyed. If *hearse* is the bed on which marriage lies dead, marriage has already been destroyed and there is no point in blighting it with further plagues.[27] Some such statement as "blights the marriage bed with killing plagues" would fit the series far better. Once more there is conflict between the immediate context mentioning plagues and so suggesting "bed of death" and the wider context, which requires "marriage bed." It is also true that to Blake the harlot was normally associated with images of death, as when he wrote in *Auguries of Innocence*:

> The Harlot's cry from Street to Street
> Shall weave Old England's winding Sheet.[28]

For me at least, *Marriage hearse*, even in the sense of "bed of death and marriage," constitutes a minor blemish. Thus with this poem, as with *Lycidas*, I believe that it is the part of wisdom to admit that imperfection may exist. Yet, other critics have admired *Marriage hearse* with evident sincerity, as when V. de Sola Pinto speaks of the "memorable pungency in the terrible oxymoron, Marriage hearse" or when D. G. Gillham says, "The word hearse . . . carries all the force of the rest of the poem. . . . Without the word the stanza might be an attack on prostitution as a disease, but its addition turns the weight of the attack on to prostitution as a symptom . . . emphasizing the alternative of love."[29]

I cannot quarrel with such statements; I can only try to understand them. It seems to me that both critics have thought deeply about the phrase *Marriage hearse* in isolation, that in isolation it does indeed carry much of the force of the rest of the poem, and that it is indeed a "terrible oxymoron." For me, however, the oxymoron, deeply moving in itself, loses much of its force, since it does not fit into the three analogies, which constitute the structure of the second half of the poem—does not fit, that is, with the perfection which characterizes the other two analogies.

I do not wish to leave the poem without a word about the analogy which is first in the series and is the key to the other two which follow. The sweep's street cry is, by Blake, connected with the pall of soot which blackens buildings. There is no logical connection, it is true, since were there no chimney sweeps, soot would still blacken buildings. But since a church should normally be bright and shining, the blackening of the building can be taken as parallel to the moral decay of the institution itself. Blake makes a connection which is emotionally and artistically fully justified and which further prepares for the connection between harlot and marriage, where the infection is direct and actual.

I can now conclude with a brief statement of the principles with which I have been working. As always, I hope they may be of use to other analysts. First, as with "blind mouthes" and "Marriage hearse," it is better to accept imperfection than to try to explain a blemish away at the cost of inconsistency. Second, with "blind mouthes" I think we have a cogent example of the ineffectiveness of negative imagery. Third, when we advance to Blake, we have a number of instances of the revelatory power of the law of least lexical contribution in semantic analysis. We have a new, second corollary to the law in the fact that, in dealing with *charter'd*, a more precise contextual suggestion is to be preferred over a vaguer one, and we also have a further instance of the first corollary—that a wider context takes precedence over a narrower one. Fourth, with both *ban* and *charter'd* we have found that evidence from earlier drafts can be corroborative of conclusions about the final text but cannot be used to contradict such conclusions. Fifth, in connection with both *charter'd* and *Marriage hearse*, we have seen how the cooccurrence associations from other utterances of the same author may be useful.

Chapter Eight
The Locus of the Literary Work

A question which is basic to the study of literature is that of where a literary work has its real existence. Is it in a human mind or minds—that of the author, the reader, or of both—does it exist only on paper, only in sound waves, or in neither? None of these questions have received really satisfactory answers and, further, appear to have received less discussion than their importance demands. The most extended and serious discussion of them known to me is in René Wellek's chapter, "The Analysis of the Literary Work of Art," in *The Theory of Literature*.[1] Wellek comes to the conclusion that the work of literature exists as a "system of norms of ideal concepts which are intersubjective."[2] I think it is necessary to disagree with this answer, though it is certainly true that Wellek is right in his criticism of many less-sophisticated attempts to solve the problem of literary locus.

We can agree that poems do not exist in writing, since poems can exist without being put on paper at all. We can agree that poems are not located in sound alone, since they can be translated from language to language, surviving changes in sounds and words. We can also agree that the poem is not something in the unknowable mind of the author; nor is it in the multifariously unknowable minds of readers. It will be my task to reexamine the problem of locus and to offer some notes on various phases of it and a tentative final answer.

An initial phase of the problem of locus is the delimitation of the role of the performer in relation to the poem proper. The distinction is usually recognized by scholars but without much attempt at careful definition. First of all, I believe that it is a reasonable assumption that all societies recognize—though not necessarily in formal statement—a distinct performer's role. This is evident even in societies where that role may be very different from what it is in our own, since all societies praise some performers and condemn others though recognizing that the poem performed by each remains the same.

What societies assign to the performer and what they reserve to the poem alone varies greatly in time and place. Thus when Leonard Bloomfield

Note: This essay was delivered before the Fifth International Congress of University Professors of English, in Edinburgh in 1961. It was published in *English Studies Today*, 3d ser. (Edinburgh: Edinburgh University Press, 1962), pp. 41–50.

collected folk tales among the Menominee, he was astonished to find that stories totally different in linguistic content were said by his informants to be versions of the same work. The literary work consisted of no more than the framework of characters and incidents. The language and all its communicative accompaniment was assigned to the performer, with consequent liberty for change at will. At the other extreme, in which as little as possible is assigned to the performer and as much as possible to the work itself, are texts in some religious traditions. Here words and even intonation (if spoken) or punctuation (if written) are preserved with the utmost jealousy from any change by performers. The shifts in roles of the performer and poem are connected with the form in which literary works are preserved in varying societies though not fully explained in this way. Great freedom for the performer is probably commoner in preliterate societies than it is with us. Yet, even in our own society, one form, to which I would extend the title of literature, is characterized by as great a variation among performances as the Menominee folk tale. This is the oral anecdote, in which only the "point" is not to be varied at will by the performer.

In contemporary Western culture, however, the dividing line between performer and poem is fairly clear and can therefore be described. With some exceptions, the dividing line is between linguistic-stylistic structure and the paralinguistic accompaniment. By this I mean that the performer is not at liberty to change plot or poetic structure, or words, sentences, sentence divisions, or even emphasis. As a result, all those parts of intonation—stress, pitch, and pause—which indicate or identify words, sentences, sentence divisions, or parts of the sentence which carry the most information are to be considered parts of the poem. That which the performer can freely change are those parts of intonation that are the signals for emotional states, and the facial and body movements which accompany speech. In saying that the performer is not free to make changes at will in the linguistic and stylistic structure of the poem, I do not mean that performers never make such changes. They do, very frequently, and quite properly. What I do mean is that a performer who varies a word or sentence from that in his text is treating the possibility of variation as a problem to be solved by evidence and to which a right answer presumably exists. When he changes and experiments with the paralinguistic accompaniment, he is building an artistic structure, not solving a problem. Consequently, he varies at will, never assuming that a single choice is the only possible right one.

One other exception to the general rule delimiting the role of the performer can also be mentioned. This is that, since much in language is recognized by society as constituting variation between equivalents, the performer is usually left to choose when he is faced with equivalences in pronunciation or even in vocabulary. Only when such equivalences affect something clearly belonging to the structure of the poem do we limit the choice of the performer. Thus we are generally free in reading prose to vary the position of stress (and consequently the vowel quality) on such a word as *justifiable*. If it is made to rhyme with *reliable* in poetry, we cannot change it to suit our individual habits.

The importance of performer and performance, for our problem of locus, is largely negative. If a distinction between performance and poem is always present, then the locus of the poem is always something else than the performance. Also, the wide variation in assignment to performance and poem indicates that poem as well as performance may be universals but only in the sense that they are found everywhere, not in that they are everywhere the same. In general, critics with a Saussurean background have gone somewhat further than these generalizations in discussing the importance of performance in its relation to poem. They have quite naturally seen a parallel to *langue* in the poem and to *parole* in the performance.[3] This is Wellek's position, for instance. It is a tempting one but in need of careful consideration. For instance, in language, according to a view once common, drifts in *parole* can result in change in *langue*.[4] Is it really true that drifts in performance can change poems? I believe that this is what is meant by calling the poem a structure of intersubjective norms. As these norms change, the poem changes. That is, each age rewrites Shakespeare in its own image. I cannot accept this very tempting view. Surely an unchanging Shakespeare exists no matter how we interpret or misinterpret him.

If we are to clarify the analogy between performance and poem, on the one hand, and *parole* and *langue*, on the other, it is profitable, as so often before, to turn aside to language at least briefly. To a linguist with a Bloomfieldian background, the equation of *langue* with a set of subjective norms, actualized in *parole*, moves *langue* dangerously close to the unknowable. I should view *langue* as a set of things which either contrast or do not contrast in a highly symmetrical fashion. Contrasts are physically different sounds which are correlated with differences in speaker-hearer behavior. When sounds or sound-structures, whether physically different or identical, do not correlate with differences in speaker-hearer behavior, the relationship is not one of contrast but of functional identity. In either case, the primary datum is behavior, and the resultant classification rests on observation of behavior. The patterns which the analyst of language abstracts from behavior are complete and self-contained in the speech habits of individuals and do not change except as one compares the common elements in different individuals or in the same individual at different periods of time. The assumption of the analyst is that once he has collected the instances of contrast on one of the levels of language, he is then able to state the pattern in terms of recurrent identities symmetrically arranged. He works, that is, from recurrent differences to recurrent identities. The finally stated pattern is *langue*; a physically observable bit of language behavior is *parole*, which must fit into the pattern of *langue*, but is never an instance of it.

Moreover, communication is not completely described in terms of *parole* and *langue* alone. In language use, or in language study, a third element, interpretation, is important. The hearer, or the linguist, makes tentative interpretations of what he hears, finally discarding those that do not please him.[5] These successive interpretations are not the same thing as *parole*, since they are conclusions about *parole*. They are not the same thing as *langue*, since, if they were, we should be forced to suppose that *langue* changes with each change in interpretation.

Poetry shows clear similarities to all three of these entities, though it also shows differences. The clearest similarities are between poetic structure and *langue*. Thus both must be reachable as abstractions from observable behavior or its results. Furthermore, both poetic structure and *langue* are characterized by a hierarchical arrangement of levels. *Langue* has the levels of phonology, morphology, syntax, style, and the additional, outside level of meaning. Poetic structure, which falls altogether within the level of style, has levels which correspond to the three levels of *langue* below that of style. Rhyme, alliteration, and assonance correspond to and make use of phonology; patterned lexical repetition corresponds to and makes use of morphology; the repeated types of construction make use of syntax. That poetry has a level of meaning reaching beyond the words and meter of the poem itself is a commonplace.

The first and most striking difference, however, is not in structure but rather in the poetic datum which corresponds to *parole*. A basic fact about literature in contrast to casual language is that it occurs in texts which are relatively permanent. These texts, of course, do not have to be written, and they may or may not be multiple. The speech acts which are the starting point in language are impermanent and multifarious. The linguist must use a large number of these acts and must compare extensively in order to arrive at his hypothesis of structure. The fact of permanence makes such wide collection and comparison unnecessary for the student of literature. He can derive hypotheses of structure quite well from the single manuscripts of *Beowulf* or *The Pearl*—rather better, perhaps, than from the multiple copies and renditions of a ballad like *Barbara Allen*.

I would suggest, then, that what occupies the position of *parole* in relation to poetry is the text. This is the primary datum, relatively unchanging so that we can return to it. The successive interpretations of it are like the successive analyses of speech acts. They are neither like *parole* nor *langue*. Thus we avoid certain uncomfortable consequences if we recognize in poetry, too, the third element of interpretation and analysis. For instance, if a reader is foolish enough to interpret "pants" in the Coleridge line from *Kubla Khan*, "As if this earth in fast thick pants were breathing," as "trousers," we do not have to suppose that his folly in any way affects either text or structure. It merely represents an example of bad interpretation. We do not have to suppose, in turn, that Shakespeare necessarily changes from age to age—it is only the interpretation which changes.

When I suggest that the primary datum, the *parole,* of poetry is a text, which may very well be unique, two further clarifying statements are necessary. First, a text is not necessarily observable behavior. It is, rather, the result of observable behavior—that of the author, in the first writing down of the poem or the first pronouncing of it. All other later performances, copies, or editions are either mechanical reproductions of this first performance or they are interpretations of it. If they are mechanical reproductions, they can be treated as constituting the same text; if they are interpretations, they are no longer part of the primary datum. Next, the statement that poetic structure can be derived from a single text would seem to cause trouble if the text is imperfect or lost; then part or all of the primary datum is destroyed, and the poem with it. Yet a scientific bibliographer can quite successfully correct imperfect texts. I think that what a bibliographer does in studying written and printed texts can be described as being made up of two kinds of activity. One is that he studies reproductions with the purpose of removing accidental variations so as to reduce multiple texts to unity. The second activity is to interpret structure, setting up structural hypotheses so as to clarify or amplify the text in accord with them.

The reader of poetry, like the hearer of language, proceeds to abstract from the primary datum with which he is faced. The abstraction gives him structure, or a hypothesis of structure, on the several levels I have mentioned, just as the hearer of *parole* abstracts a structure of *langue* on these several levels. When the reader or hearer has constructed a hypothesis of structure which satisfies him, he says he has understood the poem, or the utterance. In no sense is the act of interpretation, or the hypothesis which results, the same thing as poetic structure per se. A hypothesis is no more the thing in itself than the theory of atomic structure is the same thing as the structure of matter.

The process of abstraction and the construction of hypotheses are much the same in poetry and in language; yet there is a difference. The formation of structure-hypotheses in language must start with listening to the contrasts and identities of sounds in order to be able to identify the meaningful entities. We do not study literature without knowledge of the language in which it occurs; so identification of the linguistic contrasts and identities is only a sort of preliminary task. As a result, we recognize literary patterns in terms of recurrent identities in sequences of longer differences. The variation in procedure is of real importance for the understanding of poetic structure and why recurrences like rhyme and meter are basic to it when they are not to casual speech.

In talking earlier about the totality of the communication system, I divided it into two parallel parts: the paralinguistic system and the linguistic system proper. The paralinguistic system—the emotional intonations and body movements which accompany talking—was excluded from poetic structure and was relegated altogether to performance.

Communication activity can be cut again, however, and this cut is necessary if poetic structure is to be described. This cut has been mentioned often before but can be referred to at least briefly again, with profit. This second cut is between the lower levels of language structure, which end at the borders of individual sentences, and the upper level, which includes those items and structures which characterize the whole of discourse. The dividing line, you will note, is horizontal, whereas the difference between linguistics and paralinguistics is made by a vertical line. The upper level, that of discourse structure and analysis, I have called the area of style. As said before, it seems reasonable to suppose that there is a system of relationships, patterning, and symmetry different from the occurrence of individual words and that the study of these extended relationships is central to the study of literature.[6]

As an example of poetic structure, in relation to text, to the several hierarchical levels of structure, and to the area of style, I have chosen Robert Herrick's poem *A Ternary of Littles, Upon a Pipkin of Jelly Sent to a Lady.*

A little saint best fits a little shrine,
A little prop best fits a little vine:
As my small cruse best fits my little wine.

A little seed best fits a little soil,
A little trade best fits a little toil:
As my small jar best fits my little oil.

A little bin best fits a little bread,
A little garland fits a little head:
As my small stuff best fits my little shed.

A little hearth best fits a little fire,
A little chapel fits a little choir:
As my small bell best fits my little spire.

A little stream best fits a little boat,
A little lead best fits a little float:
As my small pipe best fits my little note.

A little meat best fits a little belly,
As sweetly, lady, give me leave to tell ye,
This little pipkin fits this little jelly.[7]

The text offers us no problems, and there are fairly clear hierarchical levels
present in the structure. They are patterns in phonology, in lexicon and grammar within the sentences, in syntax between sentences, and in meaning. In
phonology, the poem is arranged in six verses, each composed of three lines.
Each line, in turn, is a phonological phrase, set off as a unit by the intonation
pattern and the rhyme. The phrases are rendered still more symmetrical by
identical syllable counts. This phonological symmetry performs two functions
and, in doing so, furnishes linkage with the patterning on the higher levels.
First, the phonological patterning marks this utterance as a poem, not a bit of
casual utterance. Second, it segments the pieces of which the structure is
built, giving them a uniformity exploited in the larger patterns. On the lexical
and grammatical level, the patterning is shown primarily by repetition. But
this repetition also contributes to the total design, since the poem can be said
to be a symmetrical design of closely similar sentences.

Each verse has the form

A little A best fits a little B
A little C best fits a little D
As my small X best fits my little Y.

All but the A's, B's, X's, and Y's are actually repeated from verse to verse
with minimum changes or none at all. The only variation is that A is sometimes a container, with B as the contained, sometimes the reverse, sometimes
indeterminate. It is obvious that the phonological patterning shades into this
patterning and repetition in lexicon and grammatical structure; yet there is a
difference. The patterning elements are here meaningful words and constructions; the patterning elements in phonology are sounds which are without
meaning in themselves, no matter how they function in forming parts of
meaningful items. It is this meaningful quality of lexical patterning that enables this level to shade into the next, the level of meaning.

The structure just described holds without change for the first five verses.
The conclusion of the poem differs only slightly in that the second line is not
another analogy but the request for permission—"As sweetly, lady, give me
leave to tell ye." The structure of grammar and syntax now gives way to a

more generalized analogical structure, which is: as A is to B, so C is to D, so X is to Y. This structure is repeated five times, and then the application is made: as A is to B "give me leave to tell ye," so a is to b. The analogical structure is plain within the poem, since the jelly and pipkin are so repetitiously equated with all that precedes. But it is not within the poem that this analogical structure is most important. It is in the area of meaning, without which neither poetry nor language could exist, that the analogies finally reach completion, thus giving the poem a satisfactory aesthetic quality. Herrick has said over and over that he is little and that his possessions and talents are little. Characteristically, in our culture, this is the proper way of talking of one's self and one's qualities. Fitting his little self and little possessions, he sends a little gift, to which he transfers the fittingness of a small container. Further, in the second line of the last verse he quite properly suggests that the lady is at least not fat. The gift, the giver, and the lady are all gracefully, if not completely logically, described as fitting; and by implication, the relationship is described as a small, not as a great passion. Herrick has charmingly and wittily solved a recurrent human dilemma—the difficulty of paying a compliment without involving himself or the recipient too deeply.

The poetic structure is patterning which occurs in the area of style, as I have tried to demonstrate. It is not the text, though it is accessible only through the text. It is unchanging, I believe, and equally open at all times and to all students, from the same data. The analyses change, and a poem may have as many analyses as there are critics. When analyses differ, one may be right and all others wrong, or all may be wrong. They cannot all be right, unless they are mechanically translatable one into the other. Each may be right, in part, or wrong, in part. One may seem right, yet be replaced by a later one which is better. Analyses, as I have said several times, are hypotheses. As hypotheses, they are to be judged in much the same way as the hypotheses of science. They are not structure and are not to be confused with it.

A final and special kind of disclaimer should here be added. As a student of literature and language whose background is (as I have said) Bloomfieldian, I am not a mentalist. Yet, at the same time, I think it is foolish to assume an extreme antimentalist position which denies the reality of the mind. I have not said that a poem exists only in its text. I have, rather, said that it is accessible only through its text. If we wish to assume a more Platonic position, we can say that the poem has a real abode in the mind of the author and that the structure in his mind, unknowable directly, is in an iconic relation with the structure we discover from analysis of the text. We can assume this position, and, in some sense, it is necessary to do so. Yet, since the author's mind is unknowable, the reality in the author's mind is something we need only mention and forget. It is of importance only in that quite frequently, and even in sophisticated discussion, phrases like "author's intention" occur. When the discussion is naïve, they can be dismissed. When it is sophisticated, they are probably loose equivalents of "structural hypothesis derived from analysis of the text."

My essential point has been that the nature of the poem is structure and that the locus of the structure (in practical terms) is in the area of stylistics, though I have just said that it has a final and unreachable locus in the mind of the author. Structure is patterning and symmetry of such a nature that when a part of the pattern is observed, predictions are possible about the rest of it. That is, when we have read the first acts of *King Lear*, we can predict its tragic ending and thus condemn Nahum Tate for changing it. The importance of pattern and symmetry seems to me the basic assumption of that kind of linguistics which has been called structural. And if patterning is the most important characteristic of language, it is not strange that it is also important in poetry. Ultimately, all art is patterned because it is a model of a world outside itself, in which pattern is also discoverable. Art is one of the great model activities of man which he uses to clarify his understanding of the world in which he lives. Another is science. They do not seem to me to conflict, and the day when their apparent conflicts are fully reconciled will be the day when we have reached the serenity of understanding.

Part Three
Principles for Interpreting Meaning

Chapter Nine
Principles Governing Semantic Parallels

Some years ago I found myself in a discussion of the meaning of two passages in Robert Frost's poem *Bereft*. The passages were:

> Where had I heard this wind before
> Change like this to a deeper roar?

and

> Leaves got up in a coil and hissed
> Blindly struck at my knee and missed.

The questions were whether *roar* in the first passage involved a reference to a lion and whether the several verbs in the second were a reference to a snake. My opponent maintained that reference to a lion enriched the imagery of the poem. My own position was that there was indeed a snake but that the lion was unnecessary. What follows is an attempt at a justification of this position, together with an exploitation of its theoretical consequences.

First for *roar*. The notion that it must refer to a lion is certainly not required, since, though we use it in connection with the noise of animals, we also use it for the noise of wind. The Joos law—the first law in semantics—states that, in seeking a translation or paraphrase for a given item, that meaning is best which adds least to the total meaning of the context.[1] Under these conditions, it seems clear that a paraphrase "noise of wind" adds far less to the context (wind is specifically mentioned) than does "noise of lion." In spite of possible loss of a certain amount of Empson-type richness, the Joos law would seem to dispose of the lion quite effectively.

The snake is different. In the first passage one could argue that at most there was a transfer of a single lexical item, *roar*, from a discourse about lions to a discourse about wind. In the second passage four items, all appropriate to snakes, are applied to leaves. They are "got up in a coil," "hissed," "struck," and "missed."

A rough kind of calculation can be resorted to, which quickly establishes the fact that it is far more likely that a snake reference is a part of the design

Note: This essay was originally published in *Studies in Literature and Language* 1, (1959): 356–365.

than was the lion possibility. If we take any one of these items alone, such as *hiss*, we can say that it either refers to a snake or does not. The chance of a snake reference by pure chance is then one out of two. I am of course perfectly aware that an accurate weighting would be very difficult, probably impossible.[2] One way of trying to weight probabilities would be to tabulate all the nonlinguistic items to which the form *hiss* might be applied, all the way from escaping steam to an angry theatrical audience. The chance that *hiss* referred to a snake would then be one out of this whole list of possibilities. Such a count would contain a large number of objects but would not be reliable no matter how exhaustively done. The nature of language is such that we continually apply old symbols to new situations and indeed must do so if we are to talk at all. As a result, any list of items to which *hiss* might refer is necessarily open-ended and subject to growth.

But while we have a reason to suppose that the probabilities involved in deciding whether a single item does or does not refer to a snake are one out of a very large number, contradictory evidence points toward the assumption that they are one out of a very small number. Figurative language is often repeated. Thus, whoever first referred to using money to start a money-making operation as "pump priming" very probably had in mind the image of an old-fashioned hand pump. Nowadays, however, *pump priming* is used by many individuals who never saw, much less operated, a pump handle. Thus, if we are considering *hiss* alone, we could say that we would be reasonably sure that it involved reference to a snake only if we had the unlikely assurance that this instance was the first time that *hiss* had ever been used in connection with leaves. It is the fact that repetition involves loss of reference in figurative language which enables us to apply the Joos law in rejecting reference to a lion in the use of *roar*.

In the discussion which follows, I shall assume that the possibilities involved in *hiss* as a reference to a snake are one out of two. Such a figure may be arbitrary, but it will serve our purposes nonetheless. The test which is of most importance to us is not whether an individual reference is likely or unlikely but, rather, whether as references are repeated they move toward greater or less likelihood of interpretation. The arbitrary figure of one out of two is adequate for discovering the direction of movement in probabilities. Let us suppose that the lines in which we were hunting for a lion reference had been "Where had this wind shaken its mane and roared?" *Roared*, we have decided, has a 1/2 chance of occurrence "by chance," that is, without reference to a lion as a part of the design of the poem. The same figure applies, of course, to *shaken its mane* considered alone. But the probability of the two items occurring together "by chance" is only 1/4. When two such items occur, then, the probability that reference to a lion is significant is considerably increased. If three possible "lion items" occur, the possibility that they are meaningless is 1/8; if four items, the chance is 1/16. Chances of lion reference being significant go up, therefore, as the number of items increases.

If we now turn to the possible snake reference, we see that we have four "snake items." Considering these items merely as a cluster in which the only principle of ordering is that they occur together without interruption by any "nonsnake items," the chances that the passage represents a meaningful reference are 15/16, or the reverse of the statement that there is 1/16 possibility that all these items are here "by chance." This calculation is quite sufficient to establish the conclusion that it is reasonable to believe that the reference to a snake is genuine. Yet there is a second principle which we have not yet considered. Three of the items—*coil*, *strike*, *miss*—occur not merely in a cluster but in the order in which they would be found if they were applied to a snake. They are in a specific order, significant because it is that of the reference we are endeavoring to test. The number of orders is a factorial of the number of items; the number of possible orders with three items is six, or $3 \times 2 \times 1$. Order, in short, adds a significant dimension as soon as the number of items reaches three, which is simply another way of saying that it takes three trees to make a row. In our snake reference, 1/16 must now be multiplied by 1/6, giving us a final statement that, measured as we have been doing it, there is 1/96 possibility of the snake sequence occurring "by chance."[3]

We can now, I believe, state two general principles governing possible semantic parallels. First, the likelihood of the parallel being significant is approximately doubled with each additional item which is added to form or extend a cluster. Second, when a parallel involving the order of items occurs, the likelihood of significance is further multiplied by a number which is the factorial of the number of items in the parallel. These two principles were used to establish the reasonableness of the conclusion that Frost was referring to a snake as well as to leaves; the Joos law was used to reject the possibility that he was referring to a lion as well as to wind.

We can now go on to work out some of the implications of these principles. First, no single item of figurative language, no matter how strikingly picturesque, can be assumed to contain a parallel, even when it is possible to express the parallel in an exact analogical structure. For instance, suppose that I say, "I looked at the eyes of the house." It is easy to see here an analogy; *eyes* are to *face* as *windows* are to *house*. Yet since any such figurative transference may be borrowed rather than original with the speaker, the analogical statement is merely an etymological observation, not a necessary analysis of the semantic content of the utterance before us. Here a sharp and significant difference between metaphor and simile emerges. When Poe speaks of the "vacant, eye-like windows" of the House of Usher, he gives an overt statement of comparison, and the analogy becomes an accurate analysis of the semantic relationships Poe is using.[4]

These facts have a bearing on lexicography. Since it would seem to be the duty of the lexicographer to collect all examples of occurrences of words which define their possible meanings, context by context, it would seem that instances like Frost's *roar* and the possible utterance "eyes of the house," should be collected and used to define *roar* as noise of wind, and *eyes* as windows—though in these contexts only. It does not seem that it is the duty of the lexicographer to collect all instances of genuine figures of speech, that is, those instances in which a significant semantic parallel with consequent figurative transfer occurs. Thus a lexicographer would not need to collect the Poe quotation, unless he were in need of a quotation which might explain the origin of a later metaphorical use. Similarly, a lexicographer would not need the Frost lines which refer both to leaves and to a snake. An explicator of the poem, on the other hand, would be under a direct obligation to point out and establish the snake reference.

The Joos law and the importance of support in judging possible parallels add up to a unified tool of great utility in both lexicography and annotation of texts. A principle which says that any unsupported figurative or transferred occurrence of a single item is to be read with maximum redundancy can (and should) be easily expanded to read that, if conflict arises between two possible figurative uses, the one with the greatest amount of support is chosen, that with the least amount of support rejected by being read as maximally redundant.

Thus the Joos law alone—without reference to support elsewhere—disposes of the much discussed crux in *Hamlet*:

> Or to take armes against a Sea of troubles
> and by opposing end them![5]

The maximum redundancy for the unsupported *a sea of* is *a lot of*. Commentators who justify *sea* in a more literal reading by reference to possible parallels in Irish legend or Persian history are introducing unnecessary hypotheses. More interesting is a second passage from Shakespeare, which has been discussed at length by Caroline Spurgeon:

> Was the hope drunke
> Wherein you drest your selfe? Hath it slept since?
> And wakes it now to looke so greene, and pale,
> At what it did so freely?[6]

"This falls [she writes] under the main heading of 'personification,' and is so entered, but is cross-referenced under 'drunkenness,' 'clothes,' 'sleep,' and 'turning pale.'"[7] Had the passage read merely "the hope wherein you drest yourself," there could have been no real objection to reading it as a parallel with clothing, since it could be argued that *"wherein you drest your selfe"* is sufficiently extended to represent more than one item. Yet obviously the picture of drunken clothing is ludicrous and constitutes a genuine conflict. The comparison to a drunken man is founded on at least the following items: *drunk, slept, wakes, look green and pale*. The items are, furthermore, in order. There can be no doubt, even without counting the probabilities, that drunkenness is strongly supported, clothing is not. The only sensible conclusion would seem to be to reject *clothing* as an integral part of this imagery, by reading *"wherein you drest your selfe"* as no more than the equivalent of *"that you had."* Needless to say, redefinition of images by such methods would result in considerable revision of Miss Spurgeon's suggestive study of 1935.

While lack of support is generally a negative argument, leading to rejection of interpretations, the occurrence of support can often be used to establish a positive interpretation. An example is found in *Hamlet*:

> So oft it chances in particular men
> That (for some vicious mole of nature in them,
> As in their birth, wherein they are not guilty,
> Since nature cannot choose his origin)
> By the o'ergrowth of some complexion.

A typical annotation on *mole* and *complexion* in this passage is the following:

> *mole*: blemish, flaw.
> *complexion*: part of the make-up, combination of humors.[8]

The meanings given by the editor are possible, and if each item is considerd alone, each is probably most likely. Yet a glance at the *OED* will establish the modern meanings for both *mole* and *complexion* as having been current in Shakespeare's day. The chance that they could have occurred together without reference to a figure based on the appearance of the skin is only one in four. The skin comparison is not contradicted by the larger context, so that reading both *mole* and *complexion* in accord with modern usage would seem to be a reasonable conclusion.

A second direction in which to develop the implications of the principles governing semantic parallels is in the relations of smaller sequences to larger contexts. The discussion given above should have established the fact that, in general, a larger context can be expected to take precedence over a short span. It is, furthermore, clear that items consistent on a short span can occur in fashions quite irrelevant to the design of the utterance as a whole. A good example of such a short-span consistency is one I recently heard in a technical linguistic discussion. The form "VP" had occurred quite frequently, always meaning "verb phrase." One speaker said, "The VP can be . . . president," and then immediately corrected himself to "present." The larger context clearly ruled out the possibility that officers of government were the subject of discussion.

A problem exists, however. It seems necessary to assume that there must be a point at which the larger context can no longer contradict the smaller span. If there were no such point, then every instance of a part of an utterance inconsistent with the whole would have to be explained away as being essentially meaningless. Yet, since we know that many such inconsistencies are indeed real, the existence of a critical deciding point must be assumed.

It seems to me that the critical point is precisely that at which order becomes a significant part of a suspected parallel. That is, when a parallel shows three correspondences in order, the chances that the parallel is significant reach nearly fifty to one—forty-seven to one, to be exact. With two items only, order cannot enter, and the chances are only three to one that the parallel is significant. Since communication theory has pretty well established that human interpretation of language is a stochastic process in which the highest probability is always acted on as if it were a certainty, I should submit that when this sharp rise in probability is reached, we no longer question the significance of the parallel but regard it as established.

If the approximately fifty-to-one point is critical, it has implications for the parallels consisting of unordered items. With five such items, the chance that the parallel is accidental is 1-32, and only when there are six items do we pass the fifty-to-one point. I suggest, then, that the outside limit of unordered items that we disregard because of inconsistency with a larger context is five. I am aware that the suggestion is not one capable of proof, but it is not without some slight empirical support. At least in my own experience I have met one parallel involving five unordered items which is reasonable to reject because of inconsistency with a larger context; I know of no instances of such parallels with six items. The parallel I have in mind is one in which the less-dignified meaning of *seat* in "seat of learning" was consistent with four other surrounding items, the most important of which was "fundamental components," yet is one in which the setting in a serious and humorless discussion of education either prevents the reader from seeing the possible meaning or forces him to decide that it is an irrelevant accident if he does see it. Thus I should say for all parallels where the probabilities of significance are less than the critical point of approximately fifty to one that we accept them unless they are contradicted by the larger environment. Further, it is in this area of parallels capable of being contradicted by the larger environment that we find an important difference between metaphor and simile. That is, the overt statement of parallelism which constitutes simile forces the recognition of significance, where otherwise it might be rejected. As soon, however, as we pass the critical point at which a parallel can be assumed to be significant in any case, further difference between metaphor and simile becomes unimportant in calculation of probabilities.

The possibility that a parallel can be established, even though it may be inconsistent with the larger context, gives us a powerful tool for literary criticism and analysis. Literary critics have not generally, at least of late, had a very high opinion of Bret Harte's story "Tennessee's Partner," but all too often condemnation is expressed only in terms which express a subjective reaction—as when the story is called sentimental. Aside from its other faults, however, it is possible to establish, I believe, that a major portion of the story consists in an analogy inconsistent with the structure as a whole and that this inconsistency is the basic weakness. In the end of the story, Tennessee is condemned by a mob. His Partner attempts to secure his release by a pseudolegal procedure, and the attempt is rejected violently by the mob. Tennessee is then taken to a hill and hanged. His body is claimed and buried with honor by his Partner. The Partner (in delirium it is true) returns to the scene of the execution and there meets Tennessee beside the "pine on the top of the hill," "sober, and his face a-shining." One needs only to enumerate these narrative items to realize that they parallel the story of the Crucifixion. There are certainly more than three of them, and they are certainly in an order parallel to the order of events in the Crucifixion. There would seem to be no real possibility of doubting the significance of the parallel. Further, since Tennessee has been presented previously as a thorough blackguard, the inconsistency is real, even shocking.[9]

It is true that the analysis of the Harte story I have just given is often resisted by students. I need not attempt to guess why except to point out that resistance often takes the form of insisting that parallels must be measured in terms of the closeness of the items contained in them, not merely in terms of the number of items. The objection is an interesting one and leads directly to the last theoretical implication of semantic parallelism. Closeness of parallel can be quantified if an overall parallel is broken down into smaller items such that for each one it is then possible to say that the items are the same or are different. The number of items which are the same then measures the closeness of the parallel, and the number of items which are different is irrelevant. As an instance, we may use the scene in "Tennessee's Partner" in which the Partner appears before the assembled miners and attempts to buy Tennessee's freedom with his accumulation of gold dust. I have intimated that this scene is a parallel to the scene of Jesus Christ before Pontius Pilate. Stated in this un-digested form, the parallel probably does not seem very close. Broken down into its component parts it is possible to measure its closeness. Both Jesus and Tennessee are in the presence of a hostile mob. A single man intercedes for both. The means is a legal, or near-legal device. Both intercessions are rejected by the hostile mob. The four items, in short, are more than enough to establish the parallel. The items of dissimilarity are numerous enough, of course—among them is the fact that one intercessor is a powerful magistrate, the other a simple and unimportant follower; in one story the means of inter-cession is the custom of releasing a prisoner at a certain feast, the other an at-tempt at restitution of stolen property; and many more could be found. Yet it was said above that these dissimilarities are irrelevant. The reason is a simple one. All analogies and parallels involve differing things—if no difference oc-curs, we are not dealing with parallelism but with identity. Therefore all par-allels break down sooner or later, and the only measure of their closeness is how long they maintain themselves before likeness is exhausted.

The fact that it is possible to quantify and thus measure parallels is of im-portance in two ways. The first is that of most general importance, though un-fortunately it is not yet possible to solve all problems which this conclusion raises. A number of students, particularly Eugene Dorfman, have been greatly concerned with the need for establishing some kind of process for segmenting literary narrative into ultimate units which would be parallel to phonemes in linguistic analysis.[10] The attempt at segmentation has not been completely successful, at least as yet. Consequently, the fact that narrative or other paral-lels offer an opportunity for even a limited segmentation process is one of real importance. It is too soon to say how far it may lead.

About the second implication of the possibility of quantifying and measur-ing parallels, it is possible to be more specific. In the pages that have preceded, I have tried to be careful not to use language which implied that I believe that number and order of items can establish more than that a parallel was significant. A parallel can only establish that a genetic relationship exists; it cannot define that genetic relationship. As a result, it is often true that a par-allel may exist between a given utterance and more than one other utterance or event. When this happens, quantification and measurement of the two possi-ble parallels are necessary, and the proper conclusion is that the more distant parallel is to be disregarded. The death of Tennessee, for instance, bears considerable resemblance to the death of any criminal who is hanged; yet only if we find some execution which is closer to the Harte story than is the Crucifixion are we justified in assuming that this execution is the proper analogy for the story. Hunting for parallels and judging their closeness may seem a surprisingly indirect method of studying literary texts. In actuality, parallelism, overt or hidden, is one of our most powerful tools for uncovering depth meanings.

Chapter Ten
Some Points in the Analysis of Keats's *Ode on a Grecian Urn*

The critical literature on Keats's *Ode on a Grecian Urn* is enormous, and much of it is extremely penetrating. It may therefore come as a surprise to maintain that several points in the poem need further clarification and that to do so may give us not only better knowledge of the poem but also hypotheses about method which can be tested elsewhere.

The criticisms fall into three major groups: those that take up some quite minor blemishes, or possible blemishes; a very large group that discusses at great length the equation between truth and beauty; and a smaller group which gives extended, line-by-line discussion. It is one of this last group which alone takes up the difficulty in lines 28 and 29 in the possible uncertainty of the reference of the modifying phrase "That leaves a heart high-sorrowful." I know of no group of critics who take up an extended discussion of the first two lines.

Among the criticisms which take up minor flaws, the following statements are typical: ". . . the ugly repetition of sound in 'O Attic shape! Fair attitude!'"; "The last stanza enters stumbling on a pun . . . i.e. *brede:breed*"; and ". . . the obscurely intended affectation 'brede.' "[1] What is curious here is that, though these characteristics are noted by many critics, none seem to have pointed out that it is convention, rather than the nature of poetry, which makes us think them faults. Repetitions, wordplays, and inkhorn terms were characteristic of the greatest Elizabethan poets and were regarded as ornaments rather than blemishes. Keats, it seems, might have been treated a little more leniently. Equally curious is that I know of no adequate discussion of the rhymes. Earl R. Wasserman, it is true, has a good deal to say of rhyme and meter,[2] but he does not comment on these curious rhyme pairs: *unheard:endear'd; play on:tone; sacrifice:skies; priest:drest; morn:return; Pastoral:all.* Some of these rhymes are immediately explainable in terms of variant pronunciations, not strictly dialect in every instance, but pronunciations used then

Note: This paper was privately printed in *Essays in Literary Analysis* (Austin: Dailey Diversified Services, 1965), pp. 95–105. It was prepared for and formally printed in *Studies in Language, Literature, and Culture of the Middle Ages and Later*, ed. E. Bagby Atwood and Archibald A. Hill (Austin: University of Texas Press, 1969), pp. 357–366.

but not now or used then and now but with different social status. A pronunciation used then but not now is *Pastoral* with a final vowel as in *all*; one used
then and now but with lower prestige now than then is *unheard* with the same
vowel as in the present tense. One which is a matter of dialect is *on* with the
vowel of *tone*. An uncertain rhyme is that of *priest:drest*, for which a possible
basis would be Middle English variation in length, giving a simple vowel in
priest as in the related name, *Prester John*. Two rhymes remain, and these are
interesting. *Sacrifice:skies* rhyme /-ays/ with /-ayz/, a rhyme perfect except
for the single distinctive feature of voice in the final consonant. A similar
vocalic pair, in my estimation, is *morn:return*, which I interpret (in Trager-
Smith fashion) as /-orn/ rhyming with /-ərn/ in which the difference is of only
one distinctive feature, back against central. The importance of a consideration of the rhymes is twofold, doubly important in that it has been traditional
to criticize Keats's rhymes ever since the days of John Gibson Lockhart and
the attack on the Cockney School in *Blackwoods*. Here, at any rate, Keats is
not rhyming carelessly or by eye alone. He is rhyming quite exactly within a
definable tradition. The tradition is that of English popular poetry, and it is
followed by Shakespeare and proverbs like "A stitch in time/Saves nine." In
this tradition it is a rule that rhymes are acceptable if they involve no more
than one difference in distinctive features. To define Keats as a follower of
popular tradition has at least the importance of giving us a bit of further insight into the background of his poetry. It seems to me that one of the first
tasks of the critic is to examine the external characteristics of rhyme and meter
for what they can tell us of the type of literature to which the poem belongs
and the poet's reliance on sound or letter, or on tradition or experiment.

The next point of discussion is the famous conclusion, said by Harvey T.
Lyon, in his useful *Keats' Well-read Urn*, to have occasioned more debate
"than almost any other lines of English poetry."[3] Typical, though perhaps
extreme among the attackers, is Sir Arthur Quiller-Couch, who calls these
lines "an *uneducated* conclusion, albeit one most pardonable in one so young
and ardent." And T. S. Eliot likewise finds the lines a blemish: ". . . the
statement of Keats' seems to me meaningless: or perhaps the fact that it is
grammatically meaningless conceals another meaning from me."[4] It is a tiny
cavil but of some importance nonetheless that "grammatically meaningless"
is the wrong term. Eliot surely means that the statement is referentially
meaningless, or philosophically so. The Keats line is no more grammatically
unacceptable than any equational sentence, such as "Time is money." At any
rate, all such attackers are taking the sentence in the naïve, even jejune, sense
of "everything which is beautiful is true, everything which is true is beautiful." It has long been evident, however, that the lines need not be taken so lit-

erally, and, since the days of Matthew Arnold, it has been possible to see them in at least a generalized realist-idealist philosophical framework: "For to see things in their beauty is to see things in their truth, and Keats knew it . . . It is no small thing to have so loved the principle of beauty as to perceive the necessary relation of beauty with truth, and of both with joy."[5]

The most penetrating interpretation, as well as one of the shortest, at least of those I have seen, belongs to Douglas Bush: "The meaning (and the meaning of similar utterances in the letters) may be simpler than some of the explanations of it. In a world of inexplicable mystery and pain, the experience of beauty lives in particulars, and these pass, but they attest a principle, a unity, behind them. And if beauty is reality, the converse is likewise true, that reality, the reality of intense human experience, of suffering, can also yield beauty, in itself, and in art."[6] As we shall see, in some ways I disagree with this statement, but in its recognition of the relation of reality and the ideal, it is quite right. I will try to show that it is possible to give a more precisely Platonic interpretation and that such an interpretation fits closely into the structure of the *Ode*.

In idealistic philosophy, a common view of the function of art is that it is an imitation of the ideal models of things, more perfect than the imitations found in experience. The forms of art are at least partially free of mutability and accident, as Keats insists the representations of the urn are free. The ideal models shape and control the objects of experience and so must have a real existence, even though inaccessible to us. Only the artist and the mystic give us glimpses of the world of the ideal. The abode of the ideal must be, in Wasserman's phrase, "in Heaven's bourne," or even in the mind of God. In either case, it is unthinkable that ideals in heaven, or in the mind of God, could be either false or ugly. In this final realm of the ideal, Truth and Beauty are indeed one, and the urn as an object of art reminds us of the oneness. Again to quote Wasserman, the knowledge is enough, since it endows our "earthly existence with a meaning and a purpose."[7] The conclusion of the poem is not, if this is right, uneducated but highly sophisticated in Platonic philosophy, even though numerous critics have pointed out that Keats had small Plato and less Aristotle. It should be pointed out, however, that, though thus philosophically sophisticated and, even, intellectually moving, the lines represent but one view of art and one view of being.

As with discussion of conventions and rhymes, something of importance emerges for possible use elsewhere. Two views of the equation are, first, to present it as a naïve statement, not closely related to the general structure of the poem; and, second, to present it as one in accord with a set of views falling outside the poem, it is true, but giving a meaning to the statement in close and tightly knit relation to the total structure of the ode. I would maintain that in such a choice, the critic is obligated to choose the interpretation which gives the maximum of articulated structure and that it is this increase in clarity of structure which justifies the critic in going outside the poem for information. When no such increase in structural organization results, the hypothesis that outside information is relevant is to be rejected.

We can pass to two lines which have not been generally regarded as a difficulty, except by Wasserman, who makes very heavy going of them, indeed.

> All breathing human passion far above,
> That leaves a heart high-sorrowful and cloyed.[8]

Presumably most critics have decided that the reference of the second line is to "breathing human passion" on the grounds that such a reference fits better with the general structure of the poem than would one to the "more happy love" of the figures on the urn. Yet, of course, the reference can be misinterpreted since the first of the two lines is not normal in syntax and so upsets the interpreter. Here is Wasserman on these lines:

> But his next account of this area is a powerful drama of meaningful ambiguities whose struggle with each other eventually filters out the mortal from the immortal, the mutable from the immutable, beauty from truth. Fundamentally, it is a drama of syntax, for it appears that instead of continuing to coalesce opposites by absorbing one into another, Keats has stumbled into expressing the oxymoronic condition by opposing contraries: "All breathing human passion far above." . . . At first glance, like the poet himself, we do not see that he has stumbled, for the line seems inevitable enough, and the words "human passion" appear in an inconspicuous position. But the line produces not only the meaningful ambiguity nicely calculated to express the fusion of the human and the superhuman, but also a certain degree of bewilderment, which the poet seems to share. Could it mean that the passion is human and yet is far above that human passion that leaves a heart high-sorrowful? or that there is something far above human passion and it is human passion that leaves a heart high-sorrowful? At any rate the damage has been done, and out of the bewildering disintegration of the syntax comes an unexpected attention to merely human passions . . . It appears that the poet has not created the confusion, but that the unstable situation his vision created has bewildered him in the midst of his ecstacy and forced him into a direction that he did not intend or expect. The recollection of the mortal world is calling him back to his sole self and is filtering out of heaven's bourne its component parts.[9]

It is perhaps ungracious to object to a passage which gives such a powerful picture of the poet's eye in a fine frenzy rolling, but I find a weakness in this line of argument. The weakness is that of embracing what is generally regarded as a fault (here confusion in syntax) as a virtue for special reasons. The argument is like that of a critic I once read who praised the dull style of Sinclair Lewis's *Main Street* because it was an imitation of the dullness of the subject. The logical weakness is that the argument is, as the followers of Noam Chomsky would say, too powerful. If writing is good when the syntax is clear and if writing is good when the syntax is confused, then all writing is good. It would seem necessary to replace Wasserman's interpretation by a more satisfactory one, if possible.

The facts are these: "far above" is a phrasal modifier which normally comes before a noun or in the predicate position after the verb *to be*, as in "far above passion" or "ideal love is far above passion." Placed as it is in post-nominal position, ambiguity results, since it suggests an interpretation in which the copula is supplied—"All breathing human passion [is] far above," and this in turn suggests supplying a missing relative in the next line—"That [which] leaves a heart high-sorrowful and cloyed." On a short span, such an interpretation would be reasonable enough but is to be rejected as not in keeping with the rest of the poem.

We are, I think, justified in asking ourselves if any simple operation would remove the ambiguity. There is: it is the simple restoration of normal grammatical order—

Far above all breathing human passion,
That leaves a heart high-sorrowful and cloyed.

We are also, I think, justified in asking ourselves if Keats could have had any tangible reason for departing from this normal order. Again, there is a simple answer: the order used in the poem gives a rhyme with *love*.[10]

From this instance I believe that it is possible to construct a hypothesis which may have wider applicability. I think that in the production of a poem a stage occurs in which the composer makes use of internal language in normal, though perhaps fragmentary, constructions. Such internal language may, indeed, sometimes be sufficiently articulated to be cast in relatively complete and logical sentences, which are then made over into the shape presented in the final poem. Such underlying sentences can be called the immediate source sentences, and I believe that it is sometimes possible to recover them. Further, when such a source sentence is recovered, it may be used as a tool in arriving at the meaning of the poem.

The clearest cases in which it is possible to recover an immediate source sentence are those in which (as in the Keats poem) an anomaly in structure and grammar exists in the final version, and in which the anomaly is removable by a simple operation, and in which, more importantly, the removal of the anomaly results in a statement more in keeping with the total structure than is the presented version. When, as with Keats, we find a tangible reason for departing from the hypothetical source version, the hypothesis of source is greatly strengthened. There are, of course, instances in which more than one immediate source is possible. The fact that such uncertain cases exist is no reason for objecting to the general hypothesis.

It is possible to test and widen this hypothesis by application to other poems. A good testing ground can be found in E. E. Cummings's poem *Anyone Lived in a Pretty How Town*,[11] the second line of which reads ''(with up so floating many bells down).'' The line is certainly not normal language and, so, not readily understandable. It is, however, easily restored to normal English—''(with so many bells floating up [and] down).'' The restored order fits with the general structure, if we take ''bells'' to mean the *sound of bells*, as is normal enough. Support for the statement that the possible immediate source sentence fits the structure of the poem is found in the recurrence of the sound of bells in the phrase ''both dong and ding,'' used in the last verse, and itself presumably having an immediate source in *ding-dong*.

The first line of the poem is ''anyone lived in a pretty how town.'' A part of this line is very easily restored to normal language by the substitution of *someone* for ''anyone.'' There is, furthermore, an assignable reason for the use of ''anyone'' rather than *someone*. The reason is not merely that Cummings wants to disguise his statements, as it is with the second line, but that he needs *someone* later in the poem—''someones married their everyones,'' in verse 5. The second operation in this line is less sure. The phrase ''a pretty how town'' is ungrammatical in that *how* does not occur between article and noun in this fashion. The phrase could be made grammatical as either ''a pretty sort of town'' or ''how pretty a town.'' I cannot be sure which of these processes, the first of which is substitution or the second of which is transposition, is the better immediate source here. We are guessing at the meaning, of course, but at least guessing within limits.

The interesting point is that there seem to be just two processes employed by Cummings. One is transposition, as in the Keats line or in the second line of this poem. The other is substitution. Substitution may not be certain in the first line of the poem, but it certainly is in verse 3, where the phrase ''more by more'' occurs. Here, quite certainly, the function word ''by'' has replaced the expected *and*. However, we also find omissions, like the dropping of *and* in the second line and the addition of *and* in the phrase ''dong and ding.'' These can be called subtypes of substitution, the substitution of zero for an overt form, or the reverse. I believe, first, that these are two basic processes employed by poets to produce language deviant from the normal and, also, that these processes, even including deletion and addition, are the basic processes employed in cryptography.

The processes of transposition and substitution in poetry seem to be governed by at least two considerations, both in suggesting their occurrence and in making them understandable to the reader without a formal sort of crypt-analysis. One is that the replacing form in substitution must belong to the same class as the replaced form, as I proposed with the possible substitution of *someone* for "anyone" in line 1. Both are indefinite pronouns. That is, the two forms must be members of an association class. If there is no such associ-ation, the poet would be unlikely to make the substitution, and if out of mere perversity he did, the result would be unintelligible. The other consideration is extension of pattern. Verse 3 also contains the line "and down they forgot as up they grew," where in normal language "down" would not occur. It is placed here as an extension of the normal pattern "as up they grew," where the occurrence of "up" suggests an antithetical item with the first verb.

It is not my purpose to give a detailed analysis of the Cummings poem, though it would not be difficult. It is introduced here only because it is a strik-ing example of poetic reshaping and is a good demonstration of the fact that "modern" poetry is not necessarily different in kind from more conventional verse. I can point out, however, that up to now we have been dealing al-together with instances of recovery of immediate source material where the sources contribute to the meaning by making clear what was difficult or con-fused—where we have been deciphering, in fact. There is another way in which recovery of the immediate source sentence can contribute to total un-derstanding. This occurs when the final sentence is itself clear, but the imme-diate source sentence adds to or modifies the meaning.

Emily Dickinson has a poem beginning

As imperceptibly as Grief
The Summer lapsed away—

and ending

Our Summer made her light escape
Into the Beautiful.[12]

If we adopt a method based on the Joos principle, blotting out "Beautiful," which is here surprising and therefore poetical, and then hunt for the most ob-vious way of filling the blank, I think that most would agree that the answer is *memory*—at least if we disregard the tiny difficulty caused by the definite ar-ticle. It is obvious that *beauty* and *memory* are both members of the class of abstract nouns, but the suggestion is strong that they were, for Dickinson, more strongly associated still. It is not too much to suggest that, for her, memory was beautiful, an association which would fit well enough with the character of one who had withdrawn from the world. Even if the reader should reject this particular interpretation of the Dickinson poem, I hope that he would at least accept the generalization that semantic association between replacing and the replaced form might be a clue to meaning.

We can make one last generalization about the process of recovery of possible source sentences. It is that, when more than one such source can be found, a decision as to which is better is usually on the basis of simplicity. That is, the source sentence which involves the fewer changes from the presented sentence is the better. This was a principle which in part governed our suggestion that the best source sentence for the line in Keats was that which involved no more than movement of the phrase "far above." We rejected the possible reading "All breathing human passion [is] far above / That [which] leaves a heart high-sorrowful . . ." not only because it did not fit the structure but also for the secondary reason that it involved two operations rather than the one in the version we have proposed. We cut the rejected possibility off with Occam's razor.

It is time, however, to return to difficulties in Keats. The first two lines of the *Ode* are—

> Thou still unravished bride of quietness,
> Thou foster-child of silence and slow time,

The lines have been generally admired, and most of the discussion simply expresses this admiration. The following is typical, though perhaps extreme: "Never did poet strike the keynote of a poem more emphatically in his first lines; never did Keats use words with greater economy. . . . Coming down through the centuries, unravished by time, adopted by time and silence, historian of the past."[13]

Though it is very brief, the clearest bit of discussion I have found is that of W. J. Bate: "For the actual parentage of the urn was the forgotten artist working with marble. It was only afterward left to be the 'foster-child of silence and slow time,' . . . Throughout that long fostering it has become pledged as a 'bride of quietness.' But this virginal bride is 'still unravish'd,' either by the infidelity of speaking or by the marriage consummation with 'quietness' itself."[14] Bate is clearly quite right in proposing that "still unravish'd bride" indicates one whose marriage has not been consummated. This meaning is clearly that suggested by the Joos law, and it is clearly simpler to propose the bridegroom as the ravisher rather than to propose an unnecessary third party.

Thus, of Bate's alternatives, the second is the better. Yet it is not a good one, since ravishment is not a very good description of nuptials, nor is "quietness" a very likely ravisher of anyone. Nor is it a very happy suggestion that the urn will sometime become the partner of quietness and has not yet been made so in the centuries since its creation. Upon close examination, the "still unravished bride of quietness" seems to end in inconsistency in whatever sense we take it.

If we once more apply the method used with Emily Dickinson's use of "Beautiful" and blot out "bride," we find that the item which will best fit the blank is fairly accurately pinpointed. The filler must be a noun and must not be merely an animate noun but a human noun, since it is described as a person. It will also have to be feminine, since we do not ordinarily apply either *bride* or *unravished* to males. It will also have to be a reasonably young person, since surely the last suggestion wanted is that the person thus addressed is an old maid. Also, the noun will have to be one which establishes a reasonable and probable human relationship with "quietness," the other entity which is personified. *Bride* fails in fulfilling the last of these requirements, and *daughter* and *child* are two other words which would do at least as well. *Daughter* is not specifically youthful and could also be objected to because a monosyllable is needed; thus, I would finally suggest *child*, which can be either masculine or feminine and brings the necessary suggestion of youth.

In suggesting *child* as a word which has been presumably replaced by "bride," I should wish to emphasize that I am talking about thought processes, which very probably took place rapidly and even unconsciously during the process of composition. Thus I should not expect *child* to appear in a written, early draft of the poem. Its appearance would be likely only if the substitution were fully conscious and deliberate, something which seems to me rather rare in poetic composition. It seems to me likely that the phrase which first occurred to Keats was "bride of quietness," in itself a very good way of describing the urn as quiet. He also wished, presumably, to describe the bride as chaste and unspoiled by accident throughout the centuries. He then let the two ideas fall together, probably without close examination, and thus produced a confused image.

I am fully aware of possible objections to this type of discussion. One has been briefly mentioned before—that it is not necessary to take "quietness" as the ravisher. This is the view of Solomon F. Gingerich, which seems to be specially unfortunate in that he takes one of the foster parents of the next line as the ravisher. But the basic reason for taking the bridegroom as the ravisher is simplicity—a person whose function it is to complete the marriage is mentioned in the phrase. It is unnecessary to introduce another. A second possible objection is that "ravished" need not have a specifically sexual meaning—it can mean stolen away, as in "the jewel was ravished from its case." It can be the equivalent of *ravaged*, as in "ravished by war." Finally, it can mean *charmed*, as in "ravished by her beauty." A strong objection to all of these is that in cooccurrence with "bride," the sexual connotation is almost inescapable. Further, quietness is unlikely as a thief or despoiler, and to suggest that the urn is not yet charmed by quietness is absurd. Finally, to take any one of these senses of "ravished" requires a third party, and so we are back again at the argument from simplicity. A minor and quite different objection is one mentioned by Bate, that "still" may be equivalent to the adjective *quiet*, as the punctuation of one early version suggests.[15] I should here again argue from cooccurrence probabilities—*still* before a past participle will ordinarily be taken as an adverb, and, further, if "still" is an adjective, it carries less information, since "quietness" occurs immediately after. Should "still" be the adjective, however, it would weaken, but not destroy, the line of discussion I have built up. What it would remove is the notion of future ravishment, leaving merely a negative. The negative participle alone is enough to rest the discussion upon.

At this point I find it necessary to say that the lines cannot be explained away. Keats nods as well as Homer. What we have finally reached is an analogy which is something like: the unravished urn is to quietness as the unravished bride is to the groom. Stated in this form, the main weakness is clear. "Unravished" changes meaning between the two halves of the analogy, producing the confusion.

We are faced with a somewhat paradoxical situation. I feel sure that an artist as great as Keats would have removed the confusion had it come to his conscious mind. If not in his mind, are we, as students, justified in saying that "unravished" means that the marriage has not been consummated? I think we are. That is, Keats's surface meaning is clear—the urn is very quiet, it is chaste, it has not been ravaged by anything. Surely it is better for a poet to express such a set of meanings with images which do not suggest confusion. The paradox, however, is that in pursuing an analysis of images, we end with a meaning which is in the mind of the student and probably not in the mind of the author. I shall not argue in any Freudian fashion but merely state that, in my view, the meanings are in the presented text, to be discovered by the student. They are no more in human minds now than ever, as I have tried to say throughout these essays.

Why has the blemish been unnoticed and the line admired? I can only suggest that in an impressionistic reading, "unravished bride" brings with it the appropriate connotation of purity, and readers have not gone further. To my mind, at least, the inconsistency is a fault, the only major fault in the poem. It is far more truly a fault than the repetition "Attic . . . attitude" or the affectation of "brede." Nor is the gnomic conclusion a fault, since it is capable of being read so that it makes important good sense. But to say that the first two lines contain a blemish is scarcely more than to say that Keats was human, and in human endeavor faults appear in the midst of the greatest perfection. It is imperative for the critic, however, to avoid praising faults merely because they occur side by side with and surrounded by beauties. If we fall into the temptation of praising all parts of a poem equally because we admire it greatly, we pay a heavy price in blinding ourselves to the ultimate realities of both beauty and ugliness.[16]

Chapter Eleven
Two Views of Poetic Language and Meaning: The Poem as Cryptogram and as Example of Deviant Grammar

Samuel Levin is the author of an excellent article in which he compares the sentence from E. E. Cummings, "He danced his did," with a phrase used by Dylan Thomas as title and first line of a poem, *A Grief Ago*. Levin is quite right in calling each of these utterances deviant from normal speech, and he is also quite right in saying that, at least in isolation from the rest of the poems, the Thomas phrase is more poetic than the Cummings sentence. Levin goes on from these positions to suggest that both utterances were formed by revision of the normal transformational rules by which sentences are formed. For the Cummings sentence he suggests that the revision might be a rule that a noun phrase could consist of determiner and verb. His second possibility of revision is that *did* might have been shifted to the class of nouns. In either alternative, "thousands of unwanted sentences would be generated by the grammar if it were fixed to generate *he danced his did*."[1] In arriving at this conclusion, Levin mentions and rejects a third possibility, that it might be only a small subclass of verbs, which in the grammar of the poem could occur in sentences like the one in question. His reason for rejection is the difficulty of defining any such small subclass. Thus he finds the lack of poetic effectiveness in this line a result of its ungrammaticality, measured by the generation of unwanted sentences.

When Levin examines "A grief ago," on the other hand, he points out that the rules which operate against the construction are very low level and specific, rather than high level and general. The rule which prevents "A grief ago" would seem to be no more than a cooccurrence restriction of *ago*, which normally occurs with nouns of time, as in *a year ago*. To accept "A grief ago" would bring with it no more violent anomalies than *an anger ago*, *a happiness ago*, using nouns for emotional states, rather than the usual nouns for periods

Note: This essay was delivered as a paper at the Linguistic Circle of New York and published in *Style* 1 (1967): 81–91. Its original title was "Some Further Thoughts on Grammaticality and Poetic Language." It has been revised in style and cut so as to avoid material given more fully in other essays.

of time. Levin observes, quite rightly, that the fusion of the two classes of nouns in the final phrase gives "the effect of richness which such poetic sequences produce."

If all poetically deviant sentences are the result of the same rule-governed processes as those which produce normal speech, Levin's conclusions about the two lines are inescapable. I find it, however, more acceptable to argue that there are at least two classes of poetically deviant sentences. One class involves merely normal processes but carries them to extremes, giving an utterance which is new and strange. Perhaps as good an example of this kind of deviation as I can find comes from the first line of a poem by Hopkins, *Spelt from Sybil's Leaves*

> Earnest, earthless, equal, attuneable, vaulty, voluminous, stupendous
> Evening strains to be . . . night.[2]

The sequence is mildly unusual only because normal discourse does not often offer as many as seven adjectives before the noun. Yet I know of no rule which sets a fixed limit on the number of modifiers before the noun, and I think there is none. If we agree with the transformationalist position that "vaulty . . . evening strains" is derived from such sentences as *evening is vaulty* and *evening strains*, then it seems to me probable that the rarity of such long strings of modifiers is no more than the fact that there is a limit—practical, not absolute—on the amount of material a speaker can carry in his nervous system for rapid manipulation.

Another of the very nearly normal constructions by Hopkins comes from *The Caged Skylark*: "dare-gale skylark."[3] This seems to me to be a two-step nominalization, the immediate source of which is "a skylark is a **dare-gale*" (* indicates a nonexistent form). The predicate element has then been moved into prenominal position as is usual for modifiers. *Dare-gale* is closely analogous to constructions like *pickpocket*, *kill-joy*, or *pop-skull*. The only abnormality is that the nominalization is not in common use. The same might be said for Hopkins's nominal modifying compound *leafmeal* on the analogy of *piecemeal*. One need not hunt for further examples—poets can be expected to manipulate the rules of sentence generation skillfully and to be able to press them to their limits. Notice, by the way, that in using such terms as *generation* in this connection, I am not giving them the mathematical and empty sense usual with strict transformationalists. We are here talking about processes of composition, and it therefore becomes necessary to treat the ordered rules of generative grammar as, in some sense, a model of sentence formation.

It seems to me a reasonable hypothesis to say that the poet starts with a normal sentence, often fully formed and well constructed. This underlying sentence, as I have said before, need not be either written or pronounced but may be, and often is, internal and very rapidly flashed across consciousness. This underlying sentence is then modified to reach an effect in keeping with the structure of the poem. If such a hypothesis should be accepted, then the modifications would not come high up in the generative tree but very low, so low indeed as to be below the normal sentence in which the inverted tree terminates. As a result, many poetic distortions are quite special and ad hoc.

If distortions are for a special effect, it follows that they are not generally paralleled in every sentence in the discourse which is of the same construction as the one distorted. They may be stated in ordered rules, of course, but an ordered rule or set of rules which applies only to a single item is not very important. Furthermore, when a poet presents us with a distorted sentence, I think it is often possible to restore the normal sentence with which he started. Very simple examples are the two distorted sentences from *Rabbi Ben Ezra* by Robert Browning: "Irks care the crop-full bird? Frets doubt the maw-crammed beast?"[4] (I am not concerned with the nonce compounds "crop-full" and "maw-crammed.") For the construction of these questions, we may assume the rather obvious source sentences "Does care irk the crop-full bird? Does doubt fret the maw-crammed beast?" If we then assume that the presented sentences were generated by some such high-level rule as that questions are formed by reversing the order of subject and verb, we should permit such oddities as "*Wrote Browning poetry?" and "*Chase dogs rabbits?" or even the Chomskyan "Read [past tense] you a book on modern music?" If, on the other hand, the sentences were formed on the basis of the normal ones, presumably under the pressure of meter and a desire for a rhyme for "feast," then the distortion was applied only twice by the poet, and neither the poet, the reader, nor the grammarian is under any compulsion to perform the same operation on any other normal question whatever. In fact, in the same poem Browning has the normal question ". . . whom shall my soul believe?" He does not feel it necessary to construct ". . . *Shall believe my soul whom?" as in "Frets doubt the . . . beast?"

The statement that the underlying sentence is the normal question "Does care irk the crop-full bird?" is a hypothesis and therefore tentative. It is based on a number of facts, however. First, the sentence is not normal, as presented. If it were taken as normal, *irks* and *frets* would be noun plurals and subjects. The verbs would be *doubt* and *care*. *Doubt* is grammatical enough, but *care* is not the normal verbal form, the verbal form being *care for*. *Irks* is unknown as a noun, and *frets* cannot be the subject of a verb indicating a state of mind. Granted that the sentence is abnormal, is there a normal one, which would fit the context? There is, of course, in the normal question at the start of this paragraph. The last question is, Has the presented sentence been derived by rules which would admit unwanted sentences, such as *Wrote Browning poetry?* Or has the deviant sentence been produced by some simple ad hoc operation from an underlying normal sentence? The probable answer seems to me to be that there has been a substitution, not of a lexical item, but of a pattern. That is, the signal, change of position of the verb (as when *John is a man* becomes *Is John a man?*) has been substituted for the addition of the empty verb, *Does*, which is the normal question indicator.

A much more complicated example of recovery of an underlying normal utterance can be found in the poem ''nonsun blob a,'' again by Cummings.

> nonsun blob a
> cold to
> skylessness
> sticking fire
>
> my are your
> are birds our all
> and one gone
> away the they
>
> leaf of ghosts some
> few creep there
> here or on unearth[5]

If this scramble of words is rearranged, what emerges is

> Nonsun—a blob, cold fire, sticking to skylessness.
> The birds are one and all gone away.
> They are mi[ne], our[s], your[s].
> Some few ghosts of leaf creep here or there on unearth.

The hypothesis that the rearranged form is actually the underlying utterance for Cummings's poem must rest on probabilities, since I do not think there can be any absolute proof of its rightness. Yet it can be noted that only one process was applied to the presented utterance, that of rearrangement. No words were added or omitted. The only additions are punctuation and capitalization, and the required endings on the possessives when these occur in positions other than immediately before nouns. A rough measure of the probabilities can be given by pointing out that there are 32 words in the poem, in what looks like a nearly random order. If we suppose that the sequence hides one ''right'' order—that is, one which gives sense—then the chances of finding that sensible order by chance can be assumed to be represented by a fraction of one over the factorial of 32. The factorial of 32 is a very large number, indeed, and I shall not bother to calculate it. It is $32 \times 31 \times 30$ and so on, down to one. If, as is true, more than one "right" order can be found, the numerator becomes the total number of right orders. As for the fact that more than one right order is possible, note that the pronouns can be shifted in position without affecting the meaning. However, it is clear that there are few right orders and many that are wrong, so that the chances of getting a sensible order by accident are very slight; or, put another way, the probabilities that the message derived by unscrambling is genuine are very high indeed.

Distortion by creating a sort of transpositional cipher is not usually carried as far or as mechanically done as Cummings seems to have done it. However, the mechanical nature of Cummings's rearrangement here should not be used as an argument against the hypothesis that poetic deviance is often produced by modification of an antecedent normal sentence. Cummings's poem gives the appearance of having been composed by writing each word on a card and then shuffling the cards. I can find no principles of ordering, except that the cards were shuffled a verse at a time, and all sequences of the underlying utterance more than two words long seem to have been broken up. Cummings's transpositions are not only exceptionally mechanical; they are also based on written forms, since in some poems he goes as far as to rearrange the letters within words. Distortion does not have to be based on written forms. The Browning lines could easily have been reworked from the normal sequences without the intervention of writing or, for that matter, even of audible speech. The mechanical nature of Cummings's poetical distortion is a legitimate criticism of some examples of his poetic style, though he can be very effective indeed on occasion.

A second method of poetic distortion is to substitute an abnormal word for one which is expected in a given construction. A reasonably good example is the following line from Emily Dickinson: "A narrow Fellow in the Grass."[6] The expected modifier for an animate noun like *fellow* is *thin* or *slender*. *Narrow* replaces it in this collocation, and, since it is a convention of our poetry that we admire newness, the strange construction is effective. The line is instructive in another way. Before a substitution can take place, the composer has to find a term; the replaced term can be thought of as a stimulus, the replacing term as a response. Stimulus and response have to be associated in some way, or the response will not take place. In the Dickinson line, the association is obvious, since *narrow* can replace *slender* in many contexts, as in *a narrow line—a slender line* or *his resources were narrow—his resources were slender*.

An important result of the hypothesis that the poet starts with a normal utterance, which he then distorts by transpositions and substitutions, is that

when it is possible to make a satisfactory reconstruction of the underlying utterance, it is then a useful tool in investigation of meaning. The meaning recovered by the reconstruction of underlying forms may be different in different cases. Thus in the Cummings's poem the reconstructed utterance
suggests that the subject was no more than a remarkably cold and dreary
winter day. The usefulness of the reconstruction is illustrated by the fact that
two critics have proposed interpretations which seem most unlikely in the
light of the underlying utterance. One critic has seen in the poem an erotic en-
counter between a man and a woman, and a second has seen the progress of
life from birth to death.[7]

When I return to Levin's line from Thomas, I find that, though he is casting
his analysis in more Chomskyan terms than I should use, little real disagreement exists between us. He has said that Thomas has fused "state of mind"
and "time," and whether we think of such a fusion as resulting from a
revision of the rules of sentence formation or simply as a substitution resulting
from an association, we are agreed that *grief* and *time* were associated in
Thomas's mind and that the association affects the meaning. It is perhaps
worth noting that the association is not found in Thomas alone, since Swinburne groups the two terms, though with quite different results, in his line
"And *time* remembered is *grief* forgotten."[8] But perhaps a more revealing
example of substitution which affects meaning is from another phrase used by
Thomas as a title. The phrase is "Once below a time."[9] Of this poem, one
critic has said that there are "two references: one to pre-natal existence . . .
and two . . . [to] the poet's past life."[10] I am a bit skeptical and can propose a
different bit of meaning. "Below" is an obvious substitution for *upon* in the
traditional beginning of a fairy story. We can then say that the first line indicates not only that something is "below" a given time, or is past, but also
that the poem has the quality of unreality found in a fairy story.

I disagree with Levin more importantly in the analysis of his example "he
danced his did." First, to quote only this sentence takes no account of a larger
context. The whole line is "he sang his didn't he danced his did." That is,
Cummings pairs the negative and positive forms and has thus, I believe, quite
exactly defined the small subclass which Levin found difficult to define. The
class is that small group of verbs which make their negatives by adding *-n't*. I
should for this reason expect only a small set of further distortions. Cummings
might have said things like "they shouted their wouldn't, they whispered their
would," since *would* is also a negative-suffix verb. Further, in the Cummings
example, the verbs still used as verbs are of a sort which can be called repre-
sentational, like *sing* and *dance*. A later line which seemed very different to
Levin was "they sowed their isn't"; it is an extension of the pattern already
established only in the use of a different type of verb ("sowed"), not in the

use of *isn't* as a noun. When we advance to "went their came," we are still not dealing with a totally different class of verbs. *Went* and *came* are grouped together here, and they are like *did*:*didn't* in being paired opposites, though the pairing is based on direction rather than the positive-negative relation. I should say, in short, that even if we stick to an ordered-rule and transformational explanation for those verbs which are used like nouns in this poem, we can define the affected verbs as "paired-opposite verbs, either positive-negative, or directional." If so, then we have enormously reduced the number of unwanted and ungrammatical sentences which would come with these substitutions. The number of unwanted sentences is further reduced, also, by the fact that the verbs which can stand before the pseudonouns are limited. That is, I see no reason to expect a Cummings sentence like "*they boiled their disappear, they flew their devour." Finally, of course, if these strange sentences are ad hoc distortions from underlying normal sentences, in accord with the structure of the poem, then the unwanted and ungrammatical sentences that would come with incorporating these sentences into the rules of grammar are irrelevant.[11]

It would seem that the explanation of the ineffectiveness of "he danced his did" in the strict Chomskyan terms proposed by Levin is open to question. An alternative explanation would rest on the nature of the association group to which *did* and *didn't* belong. To explain adequately, we must give a possible source sentence. I think that for both halves of "he sang his didn't he danced his did," a quite possible starting point is something like "he shouted his no." The verb is one of an associational group with *say*, *whisper*, *cry*, and *sing*. *Sing*, in turn, is associated with *dance*. As for *did* and *didn't*, they are associated by form with all the negative-suffix verbs and by meaning with *yes* and *no*. The whole association group for *did* consists of words which have no lexical reference, concrete or emotional. They are what are sometimes called "empty words." As such, it is not much more than a truism to say that we do not react warmly to them and so find them not very poetic.

Yet, while it is true that the single sentence quoted by Levin is not very poetic, I hope he would agree with me that the poem as a whole is excellent. "He danced his did" alone may be empty, but it is related to a whole set of variations: *sang his didn't, sowed their isn't, reaped their same, laughed his joy, cried his grief, went their came*. The variations are built on the use of opposites and on giving twists to the familiar. The poem is certainly superior to *nonsun*, since, though distorted, the distortions are in a pattern which adds to the meaning, rather than merely conceals it.

My quotations have included not merely Cummings and Thomas but a number of more conventional poets as well. I have done so because I believe that distortion by substitution and transposition for discoverable poetic effect is a normal poetic process, not one characteristic of unconventional moderns alone. Though it is a normal poetic process, I do not believe that it is a part of the process of normal speaking; nor is it very closely analogous to it. Poetic distortion finds its analogy in another language activity which also starts with normal utterances and superimposes distortion on them for a given purpose. The analogical activity is cryptography, which also employs substitution and transposition as its fundamental processes. Yet there is a difference. When substitution or transposition is employed so that meaning is concealed, the result is a cryptogram. When either is employed to enhance meaning by achieving an aesthetic effect, the result is a poem. In these terms, *nonsun* is a cryptogram; *Anyone Lived in a Pretty How Town* is a poem.

Chapter Twelve
Figurative Structure and Meaning:
Two Poems by Emily Dickinson

The two poems discussed in this essay are "The Soul selects her own Society," and "It dropped so low—in my Regard." The two are numbers 303 and 747 in the Thomas H. Johnson edition, and the text of the first is as follows:

> The Soul selects her own Society—
> Then—shuts the Door—
> To her divine Majority—
> Present no more—
>
> Unmoved—she notes the Chariots—pausing—
> At her low Gate—
> Unmoved—an Emperor be kneeling
> Upon her Mat—
>
> I've known her—from an ample nation—
> Choose One—
> Then—close the Valves of her attention—
> Like Stone—[1]

The poem is dated by Johnson as "about 1862." There are several pencilled changes—"On" for "To" in line 3, "Obtrude" for "Present" in line 4, "On [her] Rush mat" for "Upon her Mat—" in line 8, and "lids" for "Valves" in line 11. A later fair copy, about 1864, of the first four lines rejects both suggested changes. In the *Poems* of 1890, where the poem is given the title *Exclusion*, the changes for lines 3 and 4 are adopted, and two unauthorized changes are made. "Chariots" in line 5 becomes "chariot's," and "be" in line 7 becomes "is."

The text of the second poem is as follows:

> It dropped so low—in my Regard—

Note: This essay originally appeared in *Texas Studies in Literature and Language* 16 (1974): 195–209. It had been prepared for a volume of studies in honor of Professor Margaret M. Bryant, which unfortunately did not materialize. I hope that the reprinted version, as well as the original publication, will be accepted by Professor Bryant as a token of friendship and respect of many years' standing.

I heard it hit the Ground
And go to pieces on the Stones
At bottom of my Mind—

Yet blamed the fate that fractured—*less*
Than I reviled Myself,
For entertaining Plated wares
Upon my Silver Shelf—[2]

Johnson dates the poem "about 1863." There are several changes entered in pencil, stated to have been written about "fifteen or sixteen years after the poem was written," on the evidence of handwriting. The changes were "in the Ditch" for "on the Stones" in line 3, "*flung it*" for "fractured" in line 5, and underlining of "less" in the same line. The last change is "*denounced*" for "reviled" in line 6. In the *Poems* of 1896, the poem was titled *Disenchantment*. All changes were there rejected, though Johnson adopts the underlining of "less."

"The Soul selects" (hereafter called "Soul") has certainly been the more popular of the two poems, and there have been numerous comments on it in print. I have consulted ten, and the Clendenning *Bibliography* (1968) lists three others that I have not seen.[3] In contrast, I can find only two comments on "It dropped so low." A brief survey of the printed comments on "Soul" should be instructive, since they do not reach convergence, and none (including my own) are exhaustive. The earliest comment that I have seen is by Genevieve Taggard. Miss Taggard assumes that the person to whom the poem is directed was Colonel Thomas Wentworth Higginson, the chosen "One." She says that "Emily chose, as she describes her soul doing, and then she closed the valves of her attention. It is perfectly literal."[4] It is, of course, difficult to see how a soul with valves can be thought of as "perfectly literal." More interesting is the comment that the kneeling emperor represents fame, which never sought her, but would have been rejected had it appeared.

Next in order are two brief comments in the *Explicator* for 1944–1945. The first is a query by H. E. D., who asks, "Is there a precise scientific reference, anatomical or zoological, in the last two lines? Is the allusion perhaps to the valve of the brachiopod or the mollusc? It seems not in keeping with the dominant imagery of the first two stanzas."[5]

The second is the reply of Henry F. Pommer, who answers that the valves are to be defined as in the *OED*, "one or other of the halves or leaves of a double or folding door." He cites a use of the word in accord with this meaning from Dickinson's contemporary Bayard Taylor in 1871 and says the shut door "is consistent with the earlier imagery of 'door' and 'gate,' and of persons seeking admission to the soul."[6]

Next comes a comment by Mark Van Doren, which is unfortunate both in bibliography and comments on language, but which at least demonstrates the great appeal of the poem. Van Doren was necessarily using the Bianchi-Hampson text of 1930,[7] since the Johnson edition did not appear until 1955. Thus Van Doren read line 7 as "Unmoved, an emperor is kneeling," and comments, "The grammar too is curious. It cannot be the emperor who is un-moved—quite the contrary, for he is moved by desire to enter where she is. Yet the grammar says so, and cares not if it does."[8] The verb form *is* is not Dickinson's grammar, as Johnson has made plain, and consequently the no-tion of the poet rising superior to language is baseless. In commenting on a later line, Van Doren builds further on his notion that Dickinson and the Eng-lish language are at variance. He remarks that it would be more normal to say "known her . . . to choose one. . . . But the preposition would weaken the infinitive, and so it is cast out." There is nothing in Dickinson's construction that is ungrammatical, at least for me, since it is paralleled by constructions like *"I've seen him drive a car,"* where we have a verb of perception, a pro-noun that is object of the first verb and subject of the second, followed by an unmarked infinitive. How the variant construction with the marker *to* could "weaken" the infinitive is not explained.

In commenting on the final verse, Van Doren listens to the siren voice of onomatopoeia and finds that the sound must seem, not merely an echo to the sense, but the sense itself.

> We are forced to consider how valves could in any sense be like stone. Are they the valves of the heart? Of the mind? Does attention have valves at all? And if so, is it possible to understand "Like Stone"? There is real-ly no question. The last line carries its own authority. Such a thing, so said, has to be true. All of the *n*'s in the stanza come to their climax in the ultimate word, as "valves" has matched "ample" in its vowel, the only open one anywhere in four remarkable lines. Elsewhere the utter-ance is stern and close-lipped, as if the last thinkable thing were being said. Perhaps in some terrible sense it was.[9]

If I understand this passage, Van Doren is saying that the vowels and con-sonants carry the message, without regard to whether or not the words are ap-propriate or the images accurate. The dental nasals are stated to be "stern and close-lipped." Even more close-lipped than a dental nasal (which can be pro-nounced with fully open lips) is the sequence /mp-/ of "ample," which is stated to be characterized by its open vowel. Also, twenty-two vowels occur in the last stanza. If we assume that there are nine vowels in most varieties of English, there must be some repetition in the four lines, and the occurrence of two /æ/'s is not significant. And finally, by my count, it is not open vowels that are restricted. It is close vowels. We find only one example of /uw/(in *choose*) and no example of /iy/. As a linguist colleague once remarked to me, onomatopoeia is liable to lead the critic into far left field.

Johnson, in his *Interpretive Biography*, takes the chosen "One" to be the Muse and says that the first four lines are "a motto for her own guidance, since by now she had made most of her selections, and was closing the door on the rest."[10] That is, she chooses the Muse and rejects human friendships. John Crowe Ransom does not argue in detail, but takes the chosen "One" to be God: ". . . and all that is of earth, including the beloved is withdrawn. This is a Platonic, or a Christian climax, and the last fruits of Renunciation."[11] Charles R. Anderson is more detailed:

> A surface reading of the present poem seems to make this quite simply an affair of the heart. The central stanza weights the meaning in that direction, for the pausing "Chariots" and kneeling "Emperor" certainly suggest future suitors being rejected because of the chosen One, rather than the lures of society that might distract her from her art. On the other hand this "One" may be God, as suggested by the capitalization and by the fact that her choice is possible only at spiritual maturity ("divine Majority"); finally, there is the hint of a nunnery ("Rush mat") where she waits for Him alone, the king of Heaven surely taking precedence over mere mortal emperors. Whether her devotion is to an earthly or a heavenly lover, she is "unmoved" by the petitions of all others, closing the "Valves of her attention" to them. The organic "Valves" in this climactic image make the exclusion more vital than the variant "lids" in the manuscript, mechanical doors that shut out further vision by voluntary effort. With their anatomical references, as in those arterial valves devoted to the single function of the heart, they suggest the instinctive closing off of communication in all directions except the life-giving one. To all others she turns a heart of "Stone," the shock word that makes her choice final.[12]

I think Anderson's approach is wrong at two points. First, the analyst is not at liberty to pick and choose as it pleases him among the textual variants, as he does with "Rush mat," an apparently rejected reading, while at the same time he avoids the other variant, "lids." Next, if the chosen "One" is God, who takes precedence over mortal emperors, Anderson is disregarding the later "from an ample nation." Two other interpretations are arguable—the identification of valves with arterial valves and that of the variant "lids" with eyelids. I shall return to both of these later.

In 1956 I gave an interpretation of the poem in a public lecture at the University of Virginia. The lecture was informally printed in 1965 in a collection of essays for student use. I have included most of the lecture in this volume but have omitted the Emily Dickinson passages, since they are essentially replaced by the form given in this essay.[13] At that time I was unaware of the H.E.D. query and was, of course, independent of the interpretation given by Paul Faris in 1967, described below. I treated the poem as a series of analogies, in which in each analogy one unstated term was left to be filled in by the reader. I was presenting interpretation as a type of problem solving, a view which underlies all of the essays in this volume. I did not compare the results of such problem solving—that the soul is like an oyster and the chosen "One" like a pearl—with other interpretations, which is what I shall do here.

Since the appearance of my analysis, there have been three comments on the poem, all in the *Explicator*. The first is by Paul Faris. He quotes both Van Doren and H.E.D., noting that H.E.D. does not see how bivalves can be in keeping with the earlier imagery of doors and gates. Then he goes on: "What better final image could Emily have hit on than that of an oyster or clam snapping its valves shut when intruded upon? . . . what could be more 'like Stone' than a shut oyster?"[14] Needless to say, I am in agreement with Faris, though in a number of ways I would go beyond him, building on the suggestion of "valves" that he and I both interpret in the same way.

The second interpretation is less convincing. It is by Simon Tugwell, O.P., who says, "What she is saying, on the surface, is a rather trite, comfortable truth; but she deliberately undermines it by using imagery . . . [of] incarceration and death, intentionally leaving us uncertain what to make of it . . . 'Stone' almost always has to do with death and coldness" (though he notes an exception in poem 1510).[15] "Lids" suggests closing eyes in death, and "low gate" suggests poem 712 ("We passed before a House that seemed/A Swelling of the Ground"). Finally, "Majority," in the sense coming of age, is linked with death in poem 567, where a dying person is spoken of as "He chose—Maturity—." I believe a fallacy exists in this kind of interpretation. It is that the imagery of death is not in any way integrated in the poem commented on. Father Tugwell has merely gathered uses of words linked with death in scattered references throughout all the poems. Further, one such linkage depends on adoption of the questionable variant "lids," and another relies on only one of the possible interpretations of "divine Majority."

The last *Explicator* comment is by Elizabeth Bowman. Miss Bowman is aware of my interpretation, which she quotes: ". . . the soul selects one, of whom she makes a friend, as an oyster (the thing with valves) selects a grain of sand, of which it makes a pearl." Miss Bowman does not specifically reject this idea but says that "the shut door symbolizes the closed mind. The term 'divine majority' is ironic." Miss Bowman is quite right in assuming that no one has examined the possibility that the poet is condemning the soul's behavior and that it is proper that that interpretation should be examined. She continues, "It is now probable that the 'society' is one of ideas rather than people, the rejected postulants then, being rich and powerful ideas. The last stanza presents the extreme case where the soul, with 'an ample nation' available, limits herself to only one. That such behavior could be subject to disapproval is readily apparent."[16]

This completes the list of published interpretations, as far as I know them. Our task now is to come to a verifiable conclusion as to which of the several is the best. To reach such a conclusion I believe that it is necessary that each interpretation be thought of as a semantic parallel—an analogy—for the obvious and undeniable surface meaning of the poem. The obvious surface meaning is that a human being chooses one from among many for companionship and rejects all others. The identity of the "One" is not a part of this surface meaning and will emerge, if at all, only after examination of the analogy or analogies. To judge an analogy in this fashion, the first step is the obvious one of deciding whether or not an analogy is present. This first step is easy—the soul is spoken of as having a door. Since souls do not have doors, it is clear that the language cannot be literal but is a description of the soul by drawing a parallel with something that does have doors. The first analogy is then: a house dweller selects a visitor and shuts her door against others as the soul selects a companion and refuses all others. The analogy is amply supported, since there are four items in each half: the concrete member and the abstract member. The form of the analogy is then A:B:C:D :: E:F:G:H. The minimum necessary to establish an analogy would be only four—A:B::C:D.

The next analogy is a progressive one, building on the one already established and in keeping with it. This is the usual relation between analogies in this poem: a house dweller shuts the door on visitors seeking admission as a government body rejects candidates for membership. The result is to make the house in which the soul dwells something like a capitol building.

Several critics have taken "Majority," not as choice by election, but as maturity. However, the choice by unalterable decision is mentioned in line 2, "selects." To interpret "Majority" as something unrelated to choice is therefore uneconomical.

If choice by election within a government body is the better interpretation, why is the soul thus referred to? I think that Dickinson is relying on commonly held attitudes. The mind (or soul) is commonly thought of as a microcosm, comparable to a nation, which is a macrocosm. Note Edward Dyer's line "My mind to me a kingdom is." Why should the soul's election be spoken of as divine? One reason is that the soul is itself a divine object. A second reason is that Dickinson is here a good New England individualist and democrat—her view is *vox populi, vox Dei*. I would thus reject the Bowman interpretation that the use of *divine* is ironic. There are reasons for taking the use of *divine* in the direct sense; to take it in an ironical sense would require unequivocal confirmation elsewhere in the poem, and I believe this confirmation does not exist. The meaning for "divine" that seems best is then "coming from God."

The second verse describes the dwelling as now having a low gate and, therefore, a fence. It has a mat at the door, and I think it is therefore a cottage. The analogy is: cottage dweller rejects magnates seeking admission as government body (of the preceding verse) rejects candidates for admission. The occurrence of "Chariots" and "Emperor" creates a difficulty. Occurring together they undoubtedly suggest to many readers a Greco-Roman chariot and emperor. Such an interpretation could give a curiously anachronistic image, since the fence, gate, and doormat belong to a contemporary New England cottage. *Chariot* then seems best in the meaning given by Webster, "light four-wheeled carriage with coach-box and back seats only." The emperor is then a contemporary ruler like (say) Napoleon III. The decision for a contemporary emperor is a Joos-law decision, since an ancient-modern juxtaposition would be a greater change in the context than would a consistently modern structure.[17]

The last verse is the one that offers real controversy, as the previous survey of scholarship demonstrates. I am firmly in agreement with Faris and have held the oyster interpretation for many years. A preliminary count of the points in favor of this interpretation gives—

1. Oyster is to shell as soul is to body.
2. Oyster closes its shell so that the result is like a stone as the soul closes off receptiveness with impenetrability.
3. Oyster admits one grain of sand from a whole ocean as soul admits one companion from an ample nation.
4. Oyster and shell are smaller than a cottage as cottage is smaller than a house of government. The pattern of the three verses is, then, from larger to successively smaller objects.
5. If the oyster can be accepted, then a further analogy is implied. The oyster keeps the grain of sand and makes of it a valued object, a pearl. Similarly, the soul makes the one accepted companion into a valued object, a friend.

If point 5 is accepted, it would require the direct, rather than an ironical, meaning for "divine." It is true that the pearl analogy is not overtly mentioned but is part of a total analogical structure. If the total structure is accepted, the pearl necessarily follows.

The alternative interpretations start with one suggested by Dickinson herself. In her later penciled changes, "Valves" becomes "lids." The suggestion is one of eyelids, which become closed firmly against further vision. It would then have to be true (if we do not wish to take the incongruous analogy of an eye closed after admission of a cinder) that the admitted "One" is a single visual perception or insight, perhaps of a single truth, after which the viewer remains blind to all other truth. Such an interpretation would probably demand taking "divine" in the proposed ironical sense, but since the ironical interpretation of "divine" is itself highly questionable, the ironical meaning of "divine" cannot be taken as support for either the reading "lids" or interpretation of it as meaning refusal of vision.

A question, however, immediately arises. Is the student to give automatic agreement to the author's opinion, particularly his latest opinion? I believe not, at least not automatically. First, some evidence exists that Dickinson—judging by the fair copy of verse 1—intended to reject all the changes. Second, authors can, like others, both change their minds and make errors. George Meredith's later changes, for instance, are not very happy in the text of *Evan Harrington*. It is also true that substitution of "lids" for "Valves" does not prove that the two are closely associated semantically. Both are "closers," but Dickinson may well have changed the analogy, rather than have been thinking about "lids" when she wrote "Valves."

There are at least two losses in adopting the "eyelids" interpretation. One is the loss of the pearl-friend analogy. Also, the use of terms like society, emperor, and one from a nation suggests that what is admitted is a person, not an idea or an insight. A final loss is that "Like Stone" becomes simply a vaguely generalized use of language in a poem that is otherwise characterized by tightly organized images.

A second possibility is that "Valves" means something like faucets in pipes, which shut off the flow of something as tightly as if made of stone. I find an initial difficulty in the unexplained plural of "Valves" in this view. However, disregarding the plural, the analogy is: a person turns off a flow of liquid with a faucet firmly as the soul turns off attention with valves firmly. In such an interpretation there are a good many losses.

1. There is no necessity of thinking of the faucet turner as being inside her dwelling, as in the preceding verses. If the soul is not inside her dwelling, all parallels involving entrance and admission are lost.
2. The object that flows through the pipe is a liquid, which is then shut off. Yet in the poem it is referred to as "One," the typical substitute form for a count noun, not an uncountable liquid.
3. No reason is found for the valves to be in the plural.
4. The pearl-friend parallel is lost.

The third possibility is that apparently adopted by Anderson. The soul is identified with the heart as the seat of affection, giving the following analogy: the heart admits one object, then closes its entrance valves "like stone"; the human being admits one object of affection, then closes the entrances to affection firmly. It is of course to be admitted that statements like "she hardened her heart against him like a stone" are common usages. It is also to be admitted, as not only Anderson but also Van Doren have noticed, that the heart has valves, which can be spoken of in the plural. These are points in favor of the heart interpretation, but there are losses.

1. The hardened heart does not admit and treasure something, at least if it is the anatomical heart of which we speak. In fact, a rather ludicrous picture might emerge if we should take "close the valves . . . like stone," since, at least in our day, such an interpretation might be a reference to arteriosclerosis. I am uncertain about it here, however, since the earliest recorded instance of the word *arteriosclerosis* is in the *OED* supplement, dated 1890.

2. What comes into the heart through the valves is a life-giving liquid, blood. Once again, the reference to a liquid does not fit with a count noun referred to as "One" nor, for that matter, as "One from an ample nation," which suggests a person.

3. Again, the pearl-friend analogy is lost.

The last alternative is one that springs essentially from the suggestion of Pommer that "Valves" means the two halves of a double or folding door. If we take this suggestion, then the indweller and dwelling are presumably the same as in the second verse. The analogy is then: the cottage dweller chooses to admit one, then shuts the doors against all others; the soul elects one companion, then turns her attention from all others, shutting them out firmly. The analogy is real enough, since there are four parallel items in each half. There is, however, some loss.

1. The design of downward progression in size of dwelling is lost, since the dwelling in verse 3 is no more than a repetition of that in verse 2.

2. I find no completely satisfactory explanation of the plural of "Valves." If the house is a cottage, it is unlikely to have a double entrance door. Double doors are more likely to have occurred in a parlor or dining room, in which case the admitted one is a sort of captive in a room in the house, together with the house dweller.

3. The phrase "Like Stone" is no longer a precise image but merely a generalized equivalent of *firmly*.

4. The pearl-friend analogy is not lost but is slightly weakened and transformed. One part of the pearl-friend analogy is the valuable beauty of the pearl, a parallel for dear friendship. In the "doors" in-

terpretation, the admitted "One" is perhaps a lifelong companion, but nothing is suggested about the value of the relationship.

From the series of "oyster" analogies and subanalogies, I should draw the following parallels, therefore:

1. The oyster is smaller than a seat of government or a cottage. It therefore preserves a 3-2-1 symmetrical arrangement with the other verses.
2. The oyster is an indweller in its shell as the soul is in the body.
3. The oyster is receptive when its shell is open as the soul is when its attention is not shut off.
4. The oyster has valves, which would then explain the use of a plural in the poem.
5. The valves of the oyster shut off its receptiveness by closing as the soul shuts off receptiveness by turning off its attention.
6. Before closing, the oyster "admits" one grain of sand from the whole ocean as the soul admits one companion from a whole nation.
7. When closed, the oyster is like a stone as the soul is firmly closed when attention is turned off.
8. The oyster retains the grain of sand as the soul retains the admitted "One."
9. The oyster rejects all other objects as long as its shell remains closed as the soul rejects all other postulants.
10. The oyster transforms the grain of sand into a pearl as the soul transforms the admitted "One" into a friend.

I shall not weary the reader by counting all the parallels with each of the alternative suggestions, but if we summarize for one of them—the "doors" interpretation—we have the following:

1. Progression downward in size is lost.
2. The cottager is an indweller in the cottage as the soul is in the body.
3. The cottager is receptive when all doors are open as the soul is when attention is not shut off.
4. There is no completely satisfactory explanation for the plural of valves.
5. The doors somewhere in the cottage shut off ingress (and egress) as inward-turned attention does for the soul.
6. Before closing the doors, both soul and cottager admit one individual.
7. The parallel with closed oyster is considerably weakened, since it either means merely firmly or refers to some mechanical failure, as when doors stick.

8. The cottager retains one visitor (as a captive?) as the soul retains one companion.
9. Cottager and soul shut out all others.
10. Cottager and soul transform the retained object to permanent companion.

In examining the analogies, the attempt has been to quantify the parallels and, in so doing, the method has been to break every parallel down into its smallest parts. Only by doing so can I be reasonably sure that my analyses of two possible interpretations are genuinely comparable. The results are quantifiably statable as: ten points of parallelism exist for the oyster-pearl interpretation, and three of these points are lost or weakened in the best alternative interpretation.

Since it is the nature of analogical statement that it gives implications that reach far out into many layers of meaning, I think it can be stated that the oyster-pearl interpretation bears implications of wounding and reclusiveness which fit with the known facts of Dickinson's life. It is also true that more than one interpretation of the chosen "One" is possible. What the poem presents is either a person, or something personified, or both. Thus I do not think it is necessary to be dogmatic in accepting or rejecting the interpretations that see the chosen "One" as a person, as the Muse of poetry, or even as God. All are possible. The last statement to be made about this analogical interpretation is that, like all analogies, it must be judged on the number of positive parallels, not on the occurrence of a dissimilarity. Thus it is certainly true that the oyster does not choose the grain of sand. The reason that such a dissimilarity is not a counterexample is that all analogies break down sooner or later. If an analogy does not break down, we have identity, not comparison, as I have said.

When we turn from the tightly knit poem "Soul" to the other poem, "It dropped," we find a very different type of organization, or lack of organization.

Of the two comments I have found, the first is a reasonably accurate surface interpretation. "It is irrelevant to ask what 'it' is. The point of the poem is not to rebuke the 'it,' whatever it is, for having appeared better than it was; it is, rather, to make the moral observation that when we have overestimated something, it is ourselves we blame for our initial lack of perception. An experience of self-reproach, such as this, had to be lived out, apprehended, and dismissed; it could not be dismissed until it had been given permanent embodiment in poetic form."[18]

The second comment attempts to go further. In this, the poem is read as a renunciation of unworthy human contact and that the "Anonymous delight" of human contact is "plated wares; what that mad dream [of love] now but delirium? And what are her poems—silver shelves."[19]

The inferiority of this poem to the "Soul" is in the lack of organization of the successive images and analogies. Thus, in the first verse, something "drops low," which is the language we would apply to something going down gradually, much as mercury goes down in a thermometer. But the next two lines speak of stones at the bottom of something. The analogy is at least, not to a thermometer, but to something that has stones at the bottom. I should suggest that in all of this first verse the analogy is to something going down, as in a well. It is not, however, merely the level of the water, since it is a count noun, capable of hitting the bottom, as water would not be. I can only suggest that the basic image is of a bucket in a well.

When we go on to the second verse, we find that the action now takes place indoors, presumably in a pantry or dining room, where there is a "silver shelf" of precious objects. The unnamed low-dropping object of the first verse is now "plated ware," and the implication is strong that it is something brummagem and, further, vulnerable because of its spuriousness. It is certain that any reader seeing "plated ware" in conjunction with "silver shelf" would immediately take "plated ware" to mean silver plate in contrast with sterling. If the reader does so, he finds a contradiction with the imagery of the first verse. Silver plate is no more likely to break into pieces than is sterling. The careful student will then try to find something that would fit both breakable vulnerability and spuriousness. The most spirited defense of Dickinson's consistency is one I owe to a personal communication from Professor Francine Merritt of Louisiana State University. She quotes a book on antiques (Katherine McClinton, *Handbook of Popular Antiques*) describing a now valued type of ceramic ware, luster: "Considerable lustre was made in both silver and gold, which was intended to produce the effect of plated wares. Candle sticks, goblets . . . and complete tea sets were made in both silver and gold lustres. These pieces not only resembled the plated wares, but were actually made in the old silver or Sheffield molds."

If the spurious object was then a piece of silver luster ware, its breaking is explained. But if "silver luster" is the proper meaning, then it seems to me that we are faced with recognizing another kind of fault. "Plated wares / Upon my Silver Shelf" is so strong a suggestion of silver plate that Dickinson was at least most unwise in choosing the adjective "Plated." She would have been more accurate to her supposed meaning had she said "luster wares."

But even if we get around the breakability difficulty by interpreting as "luster ware," other difficulties remain. A difficulty of location exists, first outside with a place having a bottom of stones, and then inside where silver is kept. I find no orderly progression, as from large to small, as in the "Soul," since the spurious object is simply first outside and then inside. No reason is given for taking the silver ware or luster out of the house. Nor is any explanation given for the language of the first line, which clearly represents a gradual lowering, not a fall. In short, I feel quite positive that Dickinson never fully organized this poem, leaving it more nearly as notes for composition than as finished production. And, importantly, for interpretation, in a poem in which contradictory and inconsistent imagery is repeated, no reason is given to explain away one difficulty, if the others remain.

What has been attempted is an exercise in critical method, applied to an example of two quite comparable poems by the same author, where it turns out to be possible to come to conclusions of relative aesthetic worth, based on evidence. It is possible, of course, to upset such conclusions if better evidence can be brought to bear or if an interpretation of the present evidence can be shown to be more complete, consistent, and economical than the present one. Reliance on such criteria for judging hypotheses, I need hardly say, is generally accepted in science and ought, I believe, to be accepted as applicable in the analysis of literature. Ironically, both the analyses here given meet with emotionally based resistance—the oyster-soul analogy because of the dissimilarity of the soul to a creature like the oyster and the "It dropped" interpretation because readers admire (as I do) Dickinson's poetry and so cannot bring themselves to admit that she produced an inconsistent poem. If this essay has done no more than show that it is possible to judge a poem with the mind as well as with emotional responses of pleasure or displeasure, the study has been worthwhile. It has, however, done a little more. The one poem has been steadily popular and has many times invited critics to consider its imagery; the other poem not only is less popular, but also has not invited study of its imagery. This essay has attempted to show that readers, though not practicing a rigorous or exhaustive analysis, have always felt that the imagery of "Soul" is effective and consistent. I have tried to recover that consistency in "Soul" and show that none exists in "It dropped." If the order of the one poem and the lack of order in the other are responsible for differing reactions, we have given an example, though small, of the relevance of intellectual analysis to objects of aesthetic quality.

Notes

Introduction

1. Jonathan Culler, *Structuralist Poetics: Structuralism, Linguistics, and the Study of Literature* (Ithaca: Cornell University Press, 1975), pp. 4–5. The reference to football refers to the European, not the American, game.

2. The passage comes from Elias Schwartz, "Notes on Linguistics and Literature," *College English* 32 (November 1970): 184–186, quoted in Keith Schap, "On the Role of Linguistics in the Practice of Criticism," *College English* 36 (September 1974): 119.

3. Elias Schwartz, "Rebuttal to Keith Schap," *College English* 36 (September 1974): 122.

4. Ralph C. Baxter, "Shakespeare's Dauphin and Hopkins' 'Windhover,'" *Victorian Poetry* 7 (1969): 71–75. The case is curious, since there does indeed seem to be a genetic relation between the Hopkins poem and one scene (act 3, sc. 7) of *Henry V*, but I find no justification for supposing that possible parallels scattered throughout the play were of importance in the formation of Hopkins's imagery.

1. A Program for the Definition of Literature

1. The colleague was the respected linguist, to whom I owe much, George L. Trager.

2. See "The Locus of the Literary Work," chap. 8.

3. In oral discussion of the point of view expressed here.

4. Leonard Bloomfield, *Language* (New York: Holt, Rinehart and Winston, 1933), p. 162.

5. "Poetry and Stylistics," chap. 5.

6. In his presidential address to the Linguistic Society of America, December 27, 1956, "Metalanguage as a Linguistic Problem."

2. Toward a Literary Analysis

1. Matthew Arnold, "The Study of Poetry," in *Essays in Criticism*, 2d ser. (London: Macmillan & Co., 1913), pp. 2–3. The essay was first published in 1880.

2. Martin Joos, "Description of Language Design," *Journal of the American Acoustical Society* 20 (1950): 702.

3. The linguistic controversy here cited is that between the two groups whose names for each other are *mentalist* and *materialist*. The mentalist position is now dominant; the materialist position was dominant in 1951.

4. Had this essay been written in 1975, I should have said, ". . . made by Leonard Bloomfield, Noam Chomsky, and all their followers."

5. See, for instance, the famous condemnation of Chaucer because he is not like Dante and the statement "we are to adopt a real, not a historic estimate of poetry" (Arnold, "Study of Poetry," pp. 31-32).

6. For a contrary opinion, see the first appendix to Cleanth Brooks, *The Well-Wrought Urn* (New York: Harcourt, Brace & Co., 1947), pp. 197–225. Brooks gives a spirited attack on all forms of critical relativism.

7. Ibid., p. 101.

8. The problem of discreteness is not unique in linguistics but is found in other sciences as well, notably in modern physics. Also, with the advent of transformational-generative grammar, the problem of how to arrive at discreteness is once more of concern in linguistics.

9. In this short statement of structural analysis of sounds, I am following the practices current in the fifties. They are now under attack from transformational-generative students, but I find them still relevant for the study of literature.

10. Delivered before the Linguistic Society of America, December 1949. Harris wrote an abstract symbolic grammar of a semiliterary utterance, similar to the grammar of a poem which closes this essay.

11. *The Merchant of Venice*, act 3, sc. 2. All quotations from Shakespeare in this book (with one exception) are from the folio of 1623, for which I have used the facsimile by Helge Kökeritz (New Haven: Yale University Press, 1954). The exception is one passage from *Hamlet* which appears only in the second quarto; see chap. 9, note 8.

12. W. L. Rushton proposed a passage from *Euphues and His England* as the immediate source ("Parallel Passages," *Notes and Queries*, 4th ser., 12 [1873]: 304). Rushton has been followed by the *Variorum* and by C. F. Tucker Brooke in the work cited in note 14. J. H. Hanford proposed an additional source in a poem by "W. R." ("Shakespeare and Raleigh," *Nation* 92 [1911]: 315). The poem cited by Hanford is certainly reasonably close to Shakespeare, but later scholars have not regarded the direction of borrowing as established. There have been a number of attempts to find more distant sources in Italian or other poems, all of which make use of the eye as the entry for love. These works are admirably summarized by Charles Read Baskervill in the article cited in note 15.

13. A. H. F[ox]-S[trangeways], *London Times Literary Supplement*, July 12, 1923, p. 472; and A. H. Gray, *Modern Language Notes* 42 (1927): 458–459. The two notes are independent, but both develop the idea that the rhymes suggest *lead*.

14. Richmond Noble, *Shakespeare's Use of Song* (London: Oxford University Press, 1923), pp. 45–49; and C. F. Tucker Brooke, *The Shakespeare Songs* (New York: Morrow, 1929), pp. 150–151.

15. Charles Read Baskervill, "Bassanio as an Ideal Lover," *The Manly Anniversary Studies in Language and Literature* (Chicago: University of Chicago Press, 1923), pp. 90–103.

16. *OED*, s. v. "baby," substantive, 3. "The small image of oneself reflected in the pupil of another's eye; hence *to look babies. Obs.*" A similar definition is found in the *Dialect Dictionary*, s. v. "Babby." Among the more interesting quotations from the *OED* are "1593 *Tell-trothe's N.Y. Gift 39* That babie which lodges in womens eies" and "1621 Burton *Anat. Mel.* III, ii, vi, v. (1651), 576 They may kiss and coll, lye and look babies in one anothers eyes." This use of *baby* is also referred to by K. F. Smith, who cites the commonness of such expressions as "little lass," "mannikin," or the like in many languages to refer to the pupil, and the belief that the image in the pupil is the soul of man ("Pupula Duplex," in *Studies in Honor of Basil L. Gildersleeve* [Baltimore: Johns Hopkins University Press, 1902], p. 296). L. C. John discusses the related images in Elizabethan love poetry and remarks that Cupid is not infrequently identified with the baby, though he does not mention the Shakespeare poem (*The Elizabethan Sonnet Sequences* [New York: Columbia University Press, 1938], pp. 55–57).

17. For an example of the use of tightness of organization as opposed to disorganization, and a consequent conclusion of superiority, see "Figurative Structure and Meaning: Two Poems by Emily Dickinson," chap. 12. However, the essay referred to makes no statement about the relative merit of a simple type of organization versus a complex one. At present, the only statement that can be made is that the poet should succeed in any type of organization he attempts.

3. Pippa's Song: Two Attempts at Structural Criticism

1. John Crowe Ransom, "The Concrete Universal, II," *Kenyon Review* 17 (1955): 395.

2. See "Poetry and Stylistics," chap. 5.

3. Psalms 8:2.

4. An Analysis of The Windhover: An Experiment in Method

1. The assumptions here given constitute one of the ways in which literary analysis is similar to linguistic analysis. In both the takeoff point is a large unit: in literature it is the poem; in linguistics it is the sentence. But in both the first step is to break the large unit down into its smallest constituents before studying structural relationships in detail.

2. I should now (1975) use the term *syllabic separator*, since *plus juncture* is hopelessly confusing as to whether the term refers to a physical or merely a grammatical event.

3. The bird's name constitutes the second pronunciation trap for contemporary American college students. It is, of course, to be pronounced with the vowel of *talk*

and without an *l* sound—not as in the name of the current professional football team. The first trap is that the title of the poem has a second element pronounced to rhyme with *cover*, not *over*.

4. In a later article, "'The Windhover' Revisited," I returned to the difficulty here mentioned (*Texas Studies in Literature and Language* 7 [1966]: 350–359). My colleague Thomas Harrison reminded me that, if the bird were seen between the viewer and the source of light, he would appear as a silhouette. Thus, the only possibility of meeting both the linguistic requirements and those of the optical situation is to translate as "the dappled falcon is attracted to the dawn." The correction is of importance because it forced me to modify my view of the content of the area of preliminary information for literary study, since I now had to recognize that factual information from the physical and cultural world, as well as information from language, belonged there. In the essay "Poetry and Stylistics," chap. 5, my current views are presented in detail.

5. Jonathan Swift, *Travels into Several Remote Nations of the World by Lemuel Gulliver* (London: J. M. Dent and Sons, 1940), p. 140. The passage in question occurs in the last sentence of chap. 6 of part 2, "A Voyage to Brobdingnag." The first edition was published in Dublin in 1726.

6. W. H. Gardner, *Gerard Manley Hopkins* (New Haven: Yale University Press, 1948), 1:181–182.

7. William R. Steinhoff in oral discussion of this essay when it was given as a lecture at the University of Michigan in 1955. I have not found this sense of *buckle* in dictionaries or ornithological literature, but it seems to be implied in this comment on the poem: ". . . the act of 'Buckling,' when the windhover swoops down, when its flight is crumpled" (John Pick, *Gerard Manley Hopkins: Priest and Poet* [New York: Oxford University Press, 1966], p. 71).

8. It is an amusing illustration of the truth of this statement that a colleague told me he reread this sentence several times, each time failing to understand it. Then he realized that each time he had automatically filled it out with "——let," giving "Hamlet."

9. I. A. Richards, "Gerard Hopkins," *Dial* 81 (1926): 181.

10. It is interesting that Charles T. Scott finds metrical support for the position that the title and dedication are an integral part of the poem ("Towards a Formal Poetics," *Language and Style* 7 [1974]: 97–107).

11. This essay has been challenged, a number of times sharply. I list here references for those statements in disagreement that are known to me, since the reader may wish to consult them and form his own opinions: William H. Matchett, "An Analysis of *The Windhover*," *PMLA* 72 (1957): 310–311; Robert J. Boyle, S.J., *Metaphor in Hopkins* (Chapel Hill: University of North Carolina Press, 1960), p. 90; and Hans P. Guth, *English Today and Tomorrow* (Englewood Cliffs, N.J.: Prentice-Hall, 1964), p. 151. In addition, my colleague James H. Sledd, in a paper not now available to me because it is unpublished, took issue with my hypothesis of the possible contexts for "air, pride, plume," citing such others as "he did it with an air." In my later article, I agreed with Sledd, but I no longer do so, since the evidence of pattern in the two halves of the line seems to me to outweigh uncertainty in the meaning of the individual

items ("'The Windhover' Revisited," *Texas Studies in Literature and Language* 7 [1966]: 350–359).

5. Poetry and Stylistics

1. The formulation given here is based on George L. Trager's paper "The Field of Linguistics," *Studies in Linguistics*, Occasional Paper 1 (1949).

2. Edward Sapir, "Sound Patterns in Language," *Language* 1 (1925): 37–38.

3. W. K. Wimsatt was refuting a book which maintained that the explanation of rhyme was essentially acoustic ("One Relation of Rhyme to Reason," in *The Verbal Icon* [Lexington: University of Kentucky Press, 1954], p. 166). The fact that I do not agree with Wimsatt's own explanation of rhyme does not detract from the fact that the remark quoted is most acute.

4. See "Toward a Literary Analysis," chap. 2, where the song is analyzed in detail.

5. *The Merchant of Venice*, act 5, sc. 1, line 90.

6. *Othello*, act 1, sc. 3, line 33.

7. In a previous article I gave a brief analysis of the last verse of this poem. There I pointed to the lines "Ah, Psyche, from the regions which/are Holy Land!" So far from being unskillful because the rhyme falls on a word which is ordinarily unstressed, the penultimate line seems to me the climax of the poem. The pattern of full stress on the relative, followed by pause, is one used in speech for emphasis and is so eminently proper for the keystone of Poe's tripartite arch of Greece, Rome, and the Holy Land.

8. I have elsewhere fully expressed my skepticism on onomatopoeia; see "Sound Symbolism in Lexicon and Literature," in *Studies in Linguistics in Honor of George L. Trager*, ed. M. Estellie Smith (The Hague: Mouton, 1973), pp. 142–147.

9. For further discussion, see "Some Points in the Analysis of Keats's *Ode on a Grecian Urn*," chap. 10.

10. Carl Sandburg, "Chicago Poems," in *Selected Poems of Carl Sandburg*, ed. Rebecca West (New York: Harcourt, Brace & Co., 1926), p. 31, no. 2.

11. The analogy in "harbour's eyes" is not perfectly successful. The infant may search for the mother's breast, arms, or lap but scarcely for the mother's eyes. These are the instruments of the mother's search, rather than the goal of the infant's desire. I have not mentioned this defect in the body of the essay, since it seems irrelevant to a discussion of the manner in which analogies contribute to the total meaning of the poem.

12. William Wordsworth, *The Complete Poetical Works of William Wordsworth*, ed. John Morley (London: Macmillan & Co., 1898), p. 178.

13. Professor Yalden Thompson of the University of Virginia pointed out to me—when this paper was read there—that I might well be wrong in interpreting "temples" as churches, since the Inner and Middle Temples of law are visible from Westminster Bridge. I am uncertain about the matter, but the general context still suggests to me an ancient rather than a contemporary interpretation. The point, of course, is not crucial to the total interpretation.

14. The interpretation of the sonnet here given was worked out without attention to the biographical background of composition. I have been reminded by my friend and colleague of many years' standing, Martin Joos, that Wordsworth has told us that the poem was written as he was at the beginning of a happy journey to the Continent, and we know that it was written rather shortly before his marriage. The exhilaration of the journey and the impending marriage account for the exalted mood of the poem, in which Wordsworth reveals a great deal of his feelings, perhaps more than he knew or would have wished.

6. Analogies, Icons, and Images

1. Caroline Spurgeon, *Shakespeare's Imagery and What It Tells Us* (Boston: Beacon Press, 1958), pp. 324–326. Originally published in 1935.

2. Christine Brooke-Rose, *A Grammar of Metaphor* (London: Secker and Warburg, 1958), pp. 18–19. The Friedrich Brinkmann work referred to is *Die Metaphern: Studien über den Geist der modernen Sprachen* (Bonn, 1878), which I have not seen.

3. Brooke-Rose, *Grammar of Metaphor*, pp. 24–25.

4. Ibid., pp. 24, 28.

5. Ibid., pp. 24, 73.

6. Ibid., pp. 24, 115.

7. Ibid., pp. 24, 133.

8. Ibid., pp. 24, 151.

9. See "Beyond the Sentence," in my *Introduction to Linguistic Structures* (New York: Harcourt, Brace & World, 1958), pp. 406–417; and "Poetry and Stylistics," chap. 5.

10. Brooke-Rose, *Grammar of Metaphor*, p. 206. The discussion goes back ultimately to Aristotle.

11. See "Principles Governing Semantic Parallels," chap. 9.

12. Martin Joos, "Towards a First Theorem in Semantics," a paper delivered before the Linguistic Society of America, December 29, 1953. See also his review of Eric Hamp, where he says, "The guiding principle here, in the lexicographical tradition, is the one which I appear to have been the first to formulate in public, [that] the best meaning is the least meaning, or in other words, the proper definition is the one which makes the term maximally redundant in the group of citations. This sounds queer, almost as if it were a counsel of despair; but it is in fact the principle which governs all good lexicography even though the expert workers may not have verbalized it" ("A Glossary of American Technical Linguistic Usage," *Language* 34 [1958]: 286). Joos has taken up the matter again in "Semantic Axiom Number One," *Language* 48 (1972): 257–265.

13. *Antony and Cleopatra*, act 2, sc. 2, line 228. The quotation is from the folio, though act and scene divisions are from modern editions.

14. John Donne, *The Poems of John Donne*, ed. H. J. C. Grierson (Oxford: Clarendon Press, 1912), 1:8.

15. Cf. Hans P. Guth, *English Today and Tomorrow* (Englewood Cliffs, N.J.: Prentice-Hall, 1964), p. 131.

16. *Sir Gawain and the Green Knight,* ed. J. R. R. Tolkien and E. V. Gordon (Oxford: Clarendon Press, 1930). The passage is discussed at length in my article "The Green Knight's Castle and the Translators," *Canadian Journal of Linguistics* 17 (1972): 140–158.

17. Compare the statement by J. R. Firth: "The use of the word 'meaning' is subject to the general rule that each word when used in a new context is a new word" ("Modes of Meaning," *Essays and Studies* [1951]: 151).

18. Brooke-Rose, *Grammar of Metaphor*, p. 206.

19. Curtis Hidden Page, ed., *The Chief American Poets* (Boston: Houghton Mifflin Co., 1905), p. 41.

20. John Dryden, *The Poetical Works of John Dryden*, ed. Robert Bell (London: Parker and Son, 1854), p. 101, lines 59–60. The editor remarks that all Dryden's critics "from Johnson to Scott, notice this unlucky passage with censure" (p. 99).

21. Alice Meynell, *Collected Poems of Alice Meynell* (New York: Charles Scribner's Sons, 1914), p. 13.

22. Thomas Campion, "There is a Garden in her Face," in *Renaissance Poetry*, ed. Leonard Dean (Englewood Cliffs, N.J.: Prentice-Hall, 1950), p. 40.

23. Donne, "A Valediction Forbidding Mourning," in *Poems of John Donne*, ed. Grierson, 1:50.

24. T. S. Eliot, "The Love Song of J. Alfred Prufrock," in *A Little Treasury of Modern Poetry*, ed. Oscar Williams (New York: Charles Scribner's Sons, 1946), p. 168, lines 2 and 3.

25. Francis William Bourdillon, *The Night Has a Thousand Eyes and Other Poems* (Boston: Little, Brown & Co., 1899).

26. Edgar Allan Poe, "The Fall of the House of Usher," in *The Fall of the House of Usher and Other Tales* (New York: New American Library, 1960), pp. 120–121.

27. See "Principles Governing Semantic Parallels," chap. 9.

28. O. Henry, *The Four Million and Other Stories* (New York: Airmont, 1963), p. 145.

29. Robert Frost, "The Draft Horse," in *In the Clearing* (New York: Holt, Rinehart and Winston, 1962), p. 60. The discussion can be found reported in *CEA Critic* 25, no. 5 (February 1963): 7–8.

30. See Harold G. Henderson, *An Introduction to Haiku* (Garden City, N.Y.: Doubleday Anchor Books, 1958), p. 49.

31. To be found in Cleanth Brooks and Robert Penn Warren, *Understanding Fiction* (New York: F. S. Crofts & Co., 1946), pp. 469–471. I should add that I owe a pervasive debt, not immediately manifest to my readers, to the work of Brooks and Warren. Their collection of examples and the questions they asked about them were what first called my attention to the possibility of the type of criticism I have been following for a number of years. Since my interpretations differ very considerably from theirs, they are not responsible for what is wrong; for what is right, I am happy to thank them.

32. Firth, "Modes of Meaning," p. 151.

7. Imagery and Meaning: A Passage from Lycidas and a Poem by Blake

1. In my "Linguistics Since Bloomfield," *Quarterly Journal of Speech* 41 (1955): 254–261.

2. The text used is from Frank Allen Patterson, ed., *The Student's Milton* (New York: F. S. Crofts & Co., 1936), p. 43, lines 119–121.

3. A typical example of vague paraphrase of the Ruskin passage is from William J. Grace: "An interesting example, . . . criticized by Dr. Samuel Johnson as a mixed metaphor (which it is, but who cares), is Milton's 'blind mouths' in 'Lycidas'. . . 'Blind mouths' are clergymen who are intellectually and spiritually without vision but look after their own selves, particularly their physical selves, extremely well. You could explain this indefinitely in terms of analysis, but the compressed synthesis, *blind mouths*, has hit the situation with a force that no amount of analysis could drive home" (*Response to Literature* [New York: McGraw-Hill, 1965], pp. 59–60).

4. John Ruskin, *Sesame and Lilies* (Oxford: Oxford University Press, 1918), sec. 22, pp. 44–45. The lectures making up this work were delivered in 1865. The etymologies are "bishop," from Latin (ultimately Greek) *episcopus*, meaning "a watcher"; and "pastor," from Latin *pastor*, meaning "a feeder."

5. See "Principles Governing Semantic Parallels," chap. 9.

6. Frank L. Huntley comments that the general ignorance, greed, and corruption characteristic of the London clergy exposed them to being called a "pack of hungrie churchwolves." He then goes on: "The single phrase 'blind mouths,' therefore, brilliantly scores the prelatical vices: 'blind,' meaning ignorant and undiscerning; 'mouths' intends their greed; and the two words together, their pretense" ("A Background in Folklore for the 'Blind Mouths' Passage in *Lycidas* [lines 113–131]," *Milton News Letter* 1, no. 4 [1967]: 53–55). While it is possible to agree that the ultimate background may be a reference to wolves masquerading as shepherds, it is still possible to argue that a wolf can scarcely be described as a "blind mouth."

7. The text of the poem is from William Blake, *Songs of Innocence and Experience with Introduction and Commentaries by Sir Geoffrey Keynes* (New York: Orion Press, 1967), no page numbers but references by plates, thus plate 46. The draft is from William Blake, *Blake: Complete Writings with Variant Readings*, ed. [Sir] Geoffrey Keynes (London: Oxford University Press, 1966), p. 170.

8. See the detailed statement of the levels of literary study in "Poetry and Stylistics," chap. 5.

9. *The Tempest*, act 5, sc. 1, line 90.

10. A special kind of evidence in the *Songs* is sometimes found in Blake's illustrations. In this poem, however, all that can be drawn from them is that "London" is related to "Jerusalem," since one of the illustrations is the same for both.

11. V. de Sola Pinto, ed., *William Blake* (New York: Schocken Books, 1965), p. 182. It is also interesting that de Sola Pinto compares Blake with D. H. Lawrence; both connect brutalizing immorality with poisoning of the sexual impulse.

12. For a revealing and poignant instance of the kind of force to which a young girl of the working class could be exposed, see Steven Marcus, *The Other Victorians* (New

York: Basic Books, 1966), pp. 141–147.

13. Mark Schorer, *William Blake: The Politics of Vision* (New York: Henry Holt & Co., 1946), p. 249.

14. W. J. Bate observes that "Keats begins, 'A casement ach'd' (as usual, when writing rapidly, he is forgetting his *r*'s)'' (*John Keats* [Cambridge, Mass.: Harvard University Press, 1963], p. 449).

15. The novel mentioned is by W. Karig and H. Bird, *Don't Tread on Me* (New York: Rinehart, 1954); the spellings are found at pages 76 and 289. It is not my intention to argue that Blake would actually pronounce an /r/ in such a word as *charted*. Such a pronunciation is possible when "*r*-less" dialects are in contact with dialects having /r/, as with a Virginian of my acquaintance who drops the second /r/ in *proportion* and inserts an /r/ in *love potion*. I do not have evidence to support the existence of such confusions of sound in eighteenth-century London.

16. See "Principles Governing Semantic Parallels," chap. 9.

17. David Erdman, *Blake: Prophet against Empire* (Princeton: Princeton University Press, 1954), p. 156. The contemporary quotation is also found there.

18. Blake, *Blake: Complete Writings with Variant Readings*, ed. Keynes, p. 116.

19. William Blake, *Selected Poems of William Blake*, ed. F. W. Bateson (London: Macmillan & Co., 1957), p. 125.

20. Erdman, *Blake: Prophet against Empire*, p. 126; Joseph Wicksteed, *Blake's Innocence and Experience* (New York: Dutton, 1928), p. 190; Alfred Kazin, *The Portable Blake* (New York: Viking, 1946), p. 13.

21. M. L. Rosenthal and A. J. M. Smith: ". . . parceling out for hire and profit" (*Exploring Poetry* [New York: Macmillan Co., 1955], p. 694). E. D. Hirsch blends the two readings: "'Charter'd' means, first of all, 'hired out' . . . even the streams and rivers are enslaved" (*Innocence and Experience* [New Haven: Yale University Press, 1964], p. 262).

22. David Erdman, "Blake: The Historical Approach," in *Discussions of William Blake*, ed. John E. Grant (Boston: D. C. Heath, 1961), p. 18.

23. Erdman, *Blake: Prophet against Empire*, p. 258.

24. Hazard Adams, *William Blake: A Reading of the Shorter Poems* (Seattle: University of Washington Press, 1963), p. 282.

25. Kazin: "The Prostitute curses with infection the young husband who has been with her" (*Portable Blake*, p. 16).

26. Ibid.; Blake, *Songs of Innocence and Experience*, plate 46.

27. The most clearly indicated plague is gonorrheal blindness, referred to in "Blasts the new-born Infant's tear." Commentators have been curiously silent on the reference, however. As far as I know, the only commentator who mentions the disease is S. Foster Damon: ". . . harlots . . . infected mother and child (notably with gonorrhea) which blinded the newborn babies" (*A Blake Dictionary* [New York: Dutton, 1971], p. 244, s.v. "London").

28. Blake, *Blake: Complete Writings*, ed. Keynes, p. 433.

29. De Sola Pinto, ed., *William Blake*, p. 21; D. G. Gillham, *Blake's Contrary States* (Cambridge: At the University Press, 1966), pp. 18–19.

8. The Locus of the Literary Work

1. René Wellek and Austin Warren, *The Theory of Literature* (New York: Harcourt Brace & Co., 1949), pp. 139–158.

2. Ibid., p. 157.

3. The terms come from Ferdinand de Saussure, whose work is most readily available in translation as *Course in General Linguistics*, trans. Wade Baskin (New York: Philosophical Library, 1959), pp. 13–17. I have used the French terms rather than the English "act of speaking" and "language," since the French terms are more familiar in linguistic discussion and fit better with literary material, which is often not spoken. The French work appeared in 1915.

4. The view that sound change results from drift in *parole* was held by Saussure, Sapir, and most linguists until recently. The matter is not settled, but transformational-generative analysts usually hold that sound change results from change in rules of the speaker's grammar. The matter is not very important in this context.

5. In a more modern view, one would say that the first stage of interpretation is the hearer's construction of an internal sentence, which he then matches with the spoken sentence of the speaker. This can also be spoken of as abstraction from a presented speech act, but it is done very rapidly and without reaching consciousness. Later stages, on the other hand, are often fully conscious.

6. See "Poetry and Stylistics," chap. 5, and "An Analysis of *The Windhover*: An Experiment in Method," chap. 4.

7. Robert Herrick, *Robert Herrick: The Hesperides and Noble Numbers*, ed. Alfred Pollard (London: George Routledge and Sons, n.d.), 1:59–60. A very tiny difficulty occurs in phonological structure. The rhyme *belly:tell ye* is imperfect in Modern English, but in Herrick's day it was exact. A similar treatment of the second person plural pronoun is preserved in the colloquial imperative "Looky, looky," that is, "Look ye!"

9. Principles Governing Semantic Parallels

1. See "Analogies, Icons, and Images," chap. 6, and note 12 to that essay.

2. I am indebted to my colleague R. E. Greenwood for enlightening discussion of the mathematical difficulties involved in an accurate, rather than a merely approximate, measure of probabilities of this sort.

3. The number of items here is four, but one, *hiss*, can occur in any position in the series.

4. See "Analogies, Icons, and Images," chap. 6.

5. *Hamlet*, act 3, sc. 1, lines 59–60.

6. *Macbeth*, act 1, sc. 7, lines 35–38.

7. Caroline Spurgeon, *Shakespeare's Imagery and What It Tells Us* (Boston: Beacon Press, 1958), p. 306; originally published in 1935. Spurgeon speaks almost

despairingly of arriving at consistent results in tabulating imagery: "Any count of this kind, however carefully done, must to some extent be an approximate one, dependent on the literary judgment and methods of the person who has compiled it." She continues, citing this *Macbeth* passage as evidence supporting her thesis that Macbeth is consistently presented as a man whose clothes are too big for him (p. 326). In chapter six, I cited Spurgeon's classification of images according to the types of objects they represented as generally successful; the excellence of the classification is independent of the success of individual analyses of images.

8. *Hamlet*, act 1, sc. 4, lines 23–27. The passage is not in the folio but in the second quarto. The quotation here is taken from the modern edition, which contains the cited annotation (William Farnham, ed., *William Shakespeare: The Tragedy of Hamlet Prince of Denmark* [Baltimore: Penguin Books, 1957], p. 50). I owe this example to the kindness of my student Dr. Saad Gamal.

9. I have taken up the parallels between the Bret Harte story and the Crucifixion at length in " 'Tennessee's Partner' by Bret Harte," *ELEC Publications* 8 (1967): 20-25.

10. Eugene Dorfman, "The Structure of the Narrative: A Linguistic Approach," *History of Ideas News Letter* 2 (1956): 63–67.

10. Some Points in the Analysis of Keats's Ode on a Grecian Urn

1. The first quotation comes from Samuel C. Chew, *A Literary History of England*, ed. Albert C. Baugh (New York: Appleton-Century-Crofts, 1948), p. 1249. The second is from Robert Bridges's critical introduction to *Poems of John Keats*, ed. G. Thorn Drury (London: Lawrence and Bullen, 1895), p. lxvi. The third is from H. W. Garrod, *Keats* (Oxford: Clarendon Press, 1926), p. 103. All these criticisms and many more are conveniently gathered together in Harvey T. Lyon, *Keats' Well-read Urn: An Introduction to Literary Method* (New York: Henry Holt & Co., 1958). The quotations occur there at pages 100, 47, and 60, respectively.

2. Earl R. Wasserman, *The Finer Tone: Keats' Major Poems* (Baltimore: Johns Hopkins University Press, 1953), pp. 27–29. Keats's rhymes and spellings would be worth a thorough investigation, since even standard works present rather hasty generalizations on them. See, for instance, the conclusion of W. J. Bate that Keats had some special difficulty in pronunciation of /r/, since examples of dropping the letter are common in his writing (*John Keats* [Cambridge, Mass.: Harvard University Press, 1963]; examples of "r-less" spellings are at pages 449 and 450).

3. Lyon, *Keats' Well-read Urn*, p. 6.

4. Ibid., pp. 39–41.

5. Matthew Arnold, "John Keats," in *Essays in Criticism*, 2d ser. (London: Macmillan & Co., 1913), pp. 116–117. The essay first appeared in 1880.

6. Douglas Bush, "Keats and His Ideas," in *English Romantic Poets: Modern Essays in Criticism*, ed. M. H. Abrams (New York: Oxford University Press, 1960), p. 335.

7. Wasserman, *Finer Tone*, p. 41.

8. I have used the convenient edition of Walter S. Scott, *The Poetical Works of John Keats* (New York: Macmillan Co., 1907), pp. 66–68, lines 28–29. This edition modernizes spelling slightly. Thus "ravish'd" is expanded to "ravished."

9. Wasserman, *Finer Tone*, pp. 39–41.

10. The conclusion that line 28 has an immediate source phrase in "far above all . . . human passion" seems to me to dispose of a difficulty that Kenneth Burke found (or made) in lines 29 and 30 and which I discovered only after completion of this essay. Burke makes these two lines modify the idealistic love on the urn, not human love. To do so means that he interprets "that," not as a relative, but as a demonstrative pronoun and must stress it accordingly. He also interprets "leaves" as *departs from* ("Symbolic Action in a Poem by Keats," in *A Grammar of Motives* [Englewood Cliffs, N.J.: Prentice-Hall, 1945], p. 453). Nelson Francis rightly cites Burke's interpretation as an unfortunate ignoring of syntax (*Syntax and Literary Interpretation,* Report of the 11th Annual Round Table Meeting on Linguistics and Language Teaching, monograph 13 [Washington, D.C.: Georgetown University, 1962], pp. 83–92). I have made use of the hypothesis of underlying sentences, sometimes recoverable, in "Two Views of Poetic Language and Meaning: The Poem as Cryptogram and as Example of Deviant Grammar," chap. 11.

11. E. E. Cummings, *Poems: 1923–1954* (New York: Harcourt, Brace & World, 1954), pp. 370–371. For further discussion of the poem see "Two Views of Poetic Language and Meaning," chap. 11.

12. Emily Dickinson, *The Poems of Emily Dickinson* (Cambridge: Harvard University Press, 1955), no. 1540. I owe this example to my student Professor Curtis Hayes.

13. Solomon F. Gingerich, *Beauty in Shelley, Keats, and Poe*, Essays and Studies in English and Comparative Literature, vol. 8 (Ann Arbor: University of Michigan Publications, Language and Literature, 1932), pp. 178–179.

14. Bate, *John Keats*, p. 511.

15. Ibid., n. 9.

16. After preparation of this essay for press, I saw an ingenious interpretation of the *Ode* by Darrell Mansell. He views the *Ode* as a sort of contest between the urn as an unyielding physical object and the poet's ecstatic imaginings. In line 1, it is the poet who cannot ravish the urn, to which he "has been making love. He has been wooing it with poetry." The equation of truth and beauty is a final statement by the urn, which means no more than "my beauty is someone's saying so and the truth of his saying so is that I am therefore beautiful." Needless to say, I cannot agree with these views. The interpretation of the "still unravished bride" ignores the most probable contextual meaning, and, as Mansell has said, he has arrived at the meaning of the equation without taking the total structure of the poem into account. Note his statement that the meaning "lies in whatever meaning we can derive for the two words [truth and beauty] within the statement itself rather than from somewhere outside it" ("Keats's Urn: 'On' and On," *Language and Style* 7 [1974]: 235–244).

11. Two Views of Poetic Language and Meaning: The Poem as Cryptogram and as Example of Deviant Grammar

1. Samuel Levin, "Poetry and Grammaticalness," in *Essays on the Language of Literature*, ed. Samuel Levin and Seymour Chatman (Boston and New York: Houghton Mifflin Co., 1967), pp. 224–230. The Dylan Thomas poem is from *The Collected Poems of Dylan Thomas* (New York: New Directions, 1957), pp. 63–64. The E. E. Cummings poem is from *Poems: 1923–1954* (New York: Harcourt, Brace & World, 1954), pp. 370–371.

2. Gerard Manley Hopkins, *Poems of Gerard Manley Hopkins*, Preface and notes by Robert Bridges, ed. W. H. Gardner (New York and London: Oxford University Press, 1948), pp. 104–105.

3. Ibid., p. 75.

4. Robert Browning, *The Shorter Poems of Robert Browning*, ed. William Clyde Devane (New York: F. S. Crofts & Co., 1939), p. 234, line 24.

5. E. E. Cummings, "One Times One," in *Poems: 1923–1954*, p. 389, no. 1.

6. Emily Dickinson, *The Poems of Emily Dickinson*, ed. Thomas H. Johnson (Cambridge, Mass.: Harvard University Press, 1955), no. 986; the "narrow Fellow" is a snake.

7. William Carlos Williams, quoted by Barry A. Marks in *E. E. Cummings* (New York: Twayne Series, 1954), p. 28. For the second opinion, see Marks, p. 211. I owe this example from Cummings and the critical citations to my student Dr. Betty Berutti.

8. Algernon Charles Swinburne, first "Chorus" from "Atalanta in Calydon," in *Swinburne's Collected Poetical Works* (London: Heinemann, 1927), 2:250, line 29; italics added.

9. Thomas, *Collected Poems of Dylan Thomas*, p. 147.

10. Derek Stanford, *Dylan Thomas: A Literary Study* (New York: Citadel Press, 1954), pp. 127–128.

11. It is of minor interest that Paul Roberts seems to have held the view that "he danced his did" was constructed by distortion of normal language. He states that the distortion is by transposition rather than substitution, setting up the underlying sentence as "he did his dance" (Foreword to *A Linguistic Reader*, ed. Graham Wilson [New York: Harper & Row, 1967], p. xxv). While likely enough as a solution for this sentence alone, transposition will not solve such other sentences from the poem as "went their came."

12. Figurative Structure and Meaning: Two Poems by Emily Dickinson

1. Emily Dickinson, *The Poems of Emily Dickinson: Including Variant Readings Critically Compared with All Known Manuscripts*, ed. Thomas H. Johnson, 3 vols. (Cambridge, Mass.: Harvard University Press, 1955), no. 303.

2. Ibid., no. 747.

3. Sheila T. Clendenning, *Emily Dickinson: A Bibliography, 1850–1966* (Kent: Kent State University Press, 1968).

4. Genevieve Taggard, *The Life and Mind of Emily Dickinson* (New York: Knopf, 1934), p. 12.

5. H. E. D., "Dickinson's 'The Soul Selects Her Own Society,'" *Explicator* 3, no. 3 (1944): query no. 7.

6. Henry F. Pommer, "Dickinson's 'The Soul Selects Her Own Society,'" ibid., 3, no. 5 (1944).

7. Emily Dickinson, *The Poems of Emily Dickinson*, ed. Martha Dickinson Bianchi and Alfred Leete Hampson (Boston: Little, Brown & Co., 1930), p. 8.

8. Mark Van Doren, *Introduction to Poetry* (New York: William Sloane, 1951), p. 39.

9. Ibid., pp. 39–42.

10. Thomas H. Johnson, *Emily Dickinson: An Interpretive Biography* (Cambridge, Mass.: Harvard University Press, 1955), pp. 56, 146, 246.

11. John Crowe Ransom, "A Poet Restored," in *Emily Dickinson: A Collection of Critical Essays,* ed. Richard B. Sewall (Englewood Cliffs, N.J.: Prentice-Hall, 1963), p. 95.

12. Charles R. Anderson, *Emily Dickinson's Poetry: Stairway of Surprise* (New York: Holt, Rinehart and Winston, 1960), p. 171.

13. See "Poetry and Stylistics," chap. 5.

14. Paul Faris, "Dickinson's 'The Soul Selects Her Own Society,'" *Explicator* 25, no. 8 (1967).

15. Simon Tugwell, ibid., 27, no. 5 (1969).

16. Elizabeth Bowman, ibid., 29, no. 2 (1970).

17. Martin Joos, "Towards a First Theorem in Semantics," a paper delivered before the Linguistic Society of America, December 29, 1953; and "Principles Governing Semantic Parallels," chap. 9.

18. James Reeves, "Introduction to *Selected Poems of Emily Dickinson*," in *Emily Dickinson: A Collection of Critical Essays*, ed. Sewall, pp. 121–122.

19. Ruth Miller, *The Poetry of Emily Dickinson* (Middletown, Conn.: Wesleyan University Press, 1968), p. 262.

Index